PROGRAMMING LOGIC WITH QBASIC
A Workbook of Business Programming Applications

Kristin A. Higgins
John Scott
Conestoga College

Prentice Hall Canada Inc., Scarborough, Ontario

Canadian Cataloguing in Publication Data

Higgins, Kristin A., 1956-
    Programming logic with QBASIC: a workbook of business programming applications

ISBN 0-13-328030-6

1. QBasic (Computer program language). 2. Business - Data processing. I Scott, John, 1939-
II. Title.

HF5548.5.Q33H54 1993   650'.0285'5133   C93-093568-3

© 1993 Prentice-Hall Canada Inc., Scarborough, Ontario

ALL RIGHTS RESERVED

No part of this book may be reproduced in any form without permission in writing from the publisher.

Prentice-Hall, Inc., Englewood Cliffs, New Jersey
Prentice-Hall International (UK) Limited, London
Prentice-Hall of Australia, Pty. Limited, Sydney
Prentice-Hall Hispanoamericana, S.A., Mexico City
Prentice-Hall of India Private Limited, New Delhi
Prentice-Hall of Japan, Inc., Tokyo
Simon & Schuster Asia Private Limited, Singapore
Editora Prentice-Hall do Brasil, Ltda., Rio de Janeiro

ISBN 0-13-328030-6

Acquisitions Editor: Suzanne Tyson
Developmental Editor: Lisa Penttilä
Production Editor: Willam Booth
Production Coordinator: Sharon Houston
Cover Design: Olena Serbyn

1 2 3 4 5   97 96 95 94 93

Printed and bound in Canada.

Every reasonable effort has been made to obtain permissions for all articles and data used in this edition. If errors or omissions have occurred, they will be corrected in future editions provided written notification has been received by the publisher.

Table of Contents

Preface

Overview	i
Hardware	i
Input/Output	ii
Processor - CPU	ii
Main Memory	ii
Auxiliary Storage	ii
Software	iii
Operating Systems Software	iii
Applications Software	iii
Programs	iii

CHAPTER 1 – Problem Solving

The Environment	2
Microsoft QBASIC	2
Files	2
Conventions	3
Elements of Programming	4
Solving a Simple Problem Using BASIC	5

Statement of Problem: A Sports Store Inventory:	5
Steps to Writing a Computer Program:	6
Applying the Stepwise Approach to the Sports Store Inventory Problem	7
Review Questions	12

CHAPTER 2 – BASIC Statements

Basic Statements	15
REM Statement (')	15
GOSUB and RETURN Statements	16
OPEN Statement	17
The Concept of Variables	18
Variable Types	19
INPUT Statement	20
LET (Assignment) Statement	21
PRINT and LPRINT Statements	22
DO and LOOP Statement	23
END Statement	24
Summary	24
Review Questions	26

CHAPTER 3 – Headings and Totals

Headings and Totals	31
Headings	31
Counts and Totals	33
Flowcharting	38
Review Questions	41

CHAPTER 4 – Conditional Processing

Conditional Processing	48
IF Statement	48
Relational Operators	49
Sample Logical Expressions	49
Program Logic	54
Nested IF Statements	55
Compound Conditions	59
Priority	59
Summary	60
Review Questions	61

CHAPTER 5 – Report Improvement

Improving the Appearance of Printed Reports	69
Horizontal Print Spacing	69
TAB Function:	70
SPC Function:	70
DATE$ Function	71
Print Using Statement	71
Combining Edit Masks	75
Separate Coding of Edit Masks	76
Report Layout	77
Program Design	77
Enhanced Basic Program with Edit Masks	78
Review Questions	79

CHAPTER 6 – Page Breaks

Page Breaks	82
Page Layout	82
Program Logic	83
Line and Page Counters	83
Detecting Page Full	83

Page Eject and Headings	84
Coding	84
Enhanced Pseudocode for Page Breaks	86
Enhanced Basic Program for Page Breaks	87
Review Questions	89

CHAPTER 7 – Advanced Variable Types

Advanced Variable Types	93
Numeric Types	93
Why Use Different Variable Types	95
Arithmetic and Data Types	96
Integer Arithmetic Operators	96
Integer Division	96
Practical Application of Integer Arithmetic	97
Review Questions	98

CHAPTER 8 – Group Totals

Group Totals	100
Data File Organization	101
Detecting Control Breaks	102
Group Totals	103

Report Totals – Sum of Sum Logic	104
First Attempt at Pseudocode for Program with Group Totals	105
Logic Omissions	107
False Control Break at the Start	107
Missing Last Group Total Display	108
Correct Pseudocode for Group Total Logic	109
Group Totals Program	110
Review Questions	111

CHAPTER 9 – Repetitive Processing

Repetitive Processing – Looping	118
Controlled Loops	118
DO / LOOP	118
WHILE / WEND	120
Counted Loops	120
FOR/ NEXT	121
Nested Loops	123
Summary	123
Review Questions	124

CHAPTER 10 – Interactive Programming

Interactive Programming	127
Prompting the User for Input	128
Formatted Screens	129
Basic Statements for Screen Painting	129
Examples	131
Sample Formatted Screen	132
Program To Paint the Screen	132
Input Editing on a Formatted Screen	133
Pseudocode	134
Discussion of Code	135
Review Questions	136

CHAPTER 11 – Array Processing

Array Processing	138
Dimensioning an Array	139
Referencing Individual Elements in an Array	140
Common Applications of Arrays	141
Arrays Used for Lookup	143
Loading the Arrays	143

Searching the Arrays	144
Coding a Search (Table Lookup)	145
Review Questions	147

CHAPTER 12 – String Manipulation

String Manipulation	152
LEFT$ Function	152
RIGHT$ Function	152
MID$ Function	153
LEN Function	154
INSTR Function	154
STRING$ Function	155
SPACE$ Function	155
Concatenation	155
LINE INPUT Statement	156
Numeric Functions and String Functions	157
Review Questions	158

Appendicies

Appendix I – BASIC Reserved Words	161
Appendix II – ASCII Character Codes	162
– Line Draw Characters	162
Appendix III – The QBASIC System	163

PREFACE

Overview

This text will be used for Introductory Programming - Basic, a first year Computer Programmer/Analyst course. Through the use of QBASIC the student will produce computer programs with a business orientation. Emphasis is placed on structured programming techniques avoiding the use of GOTO statements. Sequential data files will be the main source of input for the report programs. Interactive programming will also be covered, with emphasis on editing data for valid user input.

Hardware

Hardware is the physical portion of the computer system. In this book, we shall consider the IBM Personal Computer as our hardware. The personal computers are networked together. Networking allows each machine to access data stored on a common hard disk, and also allows many users to share expensive resources such as laser printers.

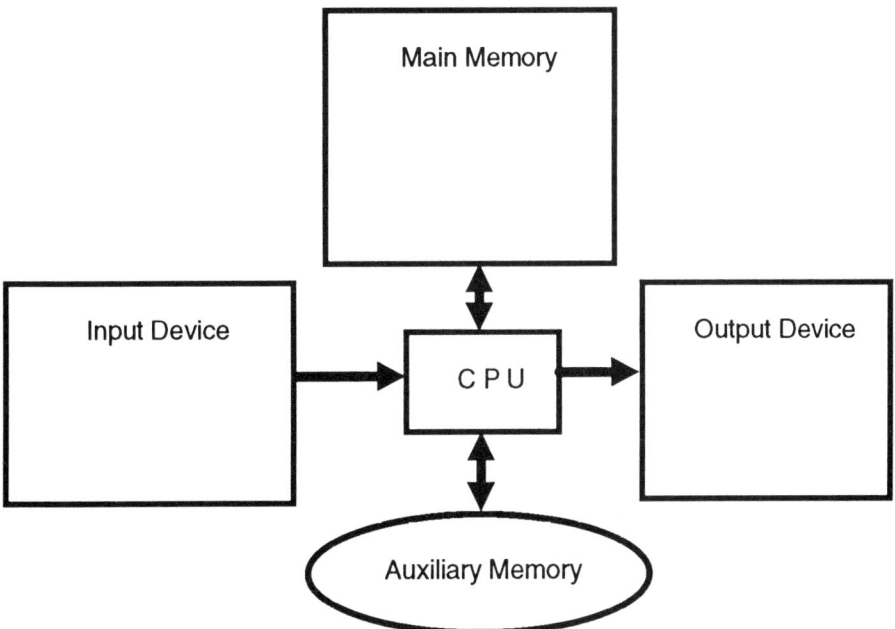

Input/Output

Input devices allow the user to enter data, programs and commands into the computer. Our standard input device is the keyboard which resembles a typewriter keyboard, with some additions. Function Keys (F1 to F12), a numeric keypad, and control keys are extra features you will find on most computer keyboards. A joystick, mouse, and voice recognition are examples of other input sources.

Output devices are used to see the results of processing. Common output devices are printers and monitors. Printers generate hard copy output. It is called hard copy because you can touch it and take it away with you. The monitor generates what is called soft copy output; output that you can see, but does not have a physical presence.

Processor - CPU

This portion of the computer hardware is commonly called the Central Processing Unit, or CPU for short. It contains the electronic components and circuitry necessary to execute instructions. This is the controlling device in the computer, since it interprets and carries out the instructions stored in the main memory of the computer. All information processed by the computer passes through the CPU

Main Memory

Main Memory, or Internal Memory, is used to temporarily hold the programs and data that are currently being used. It is important to note that Main Memory is only temporary. It is volatile, meaning that when the power goes off, all contents of main memory will be lost. For this reason you must be sure to SAVE a program you are entering or maintaining onto auxiliary storage before ending the session.

Auxiliary Storage

Auxiliary Storage (also called secondary storage) is used to store data and programs that the user wishes to keep for later use. Auxiliary storage may be thought of as long-term storage, somewhat like a filing cabinet to store large quantities of information. The most common device for auxiliary storage on a micro computer is a disk drive. There are two types of disk drives; hard disk drives, which contain non-removable disks, and floppy disk drives, into which the user may insert removable diskettes. For long term storage of program and data files you use floppy diskettes or a hard drive.

Software

Computer software is the collection of programs that makes the computer work. Software may be divided into Operating Systems Software and Applications Software. This text concentrates on Applications Software.

Operating Systems Software

This is the series of programs that controls the actual operations of the computer, such as input, output, and memory management. The operating system software used in this text is **DOS** – short for **Disk Operating System**. DOS is loaded into main memory when the computer is turned on, and resides there for the duration of a session.

Applications Software

This is software designed to perform a specific task. You will be writing application programs using QBASIC in this course.

Programs

The computer needs a set of instructions to accomplish a task.

The instructions the machine understands are in machine language and consist of binary numbers. They are generally not understandable to people. The language that we use to communicate with the computer is called a high level language. High level languages are English-like and therefore understandable by humans. Since the machine does not understand the High Level language directly, we use a compiler or interpreter to translate to machine language.

Instruction in High Level Language (Program) Source Code ⟶ Compiler or Interpreter ⟶ Machine Language (Program) Executable Code

A compiler or interpreter therefore allows humans to instruct the computer in a language that is relatively easy to write and understand, and have it translated into complex, rather obscure binary code that a computer can understand. The compiler/interpreter acts as a bridge between the human and the machine.

We write the high level instructions in the form of statements. A statement is a line of instructions that directs the machine to perform some action. For example:

    PRINT "HI THERE WORLD"

This statement, in itself a simple one-line program, instructs the computer to display the phrase inside of the quotes on the computer monitor when the program is executed.

The three things you must learn in order to write programs in High Level Language are:

1) The statements provided by the language.

2) The syntax or rules of punctuation for each statement.

3) How to assemble the statements into the correct sequence of instructions so that a problem is solved. This is often known as Program Logic.

A program is simply a collection of statements in a correct sequence.

CHAPTER 1

Problem Solving

The Environment	2
Microsoft QBASIC	2
Files	2
Conventions	3
Elements of Programming	4
Solving a Simple Problem Using BASIC	5
Statement of Problem: A Sports Store Inventory	5
Steps in Writing a Computer Program	6
Applying the Stepwise Approach to the Sports Store Inventory	7
Review Questions	12

The Environment

Microsoft QBASIC

A program is just a list of instructions to the computer to perform a given task. BASIC – Beginners' All-purpose Symbolic Instruction Code – is a programming language that is simple to use, yet powerful enough to accomplish more sophisticated tasks. There are many versions of the Basic language in existence today, each differing slightly in the syntax and options available. You will be using QBASIC in this course. **Refer to Appendix III for QBASIC commands.**

QBASIC is an environment that enables you to:

FILE LOAD	bring a file from auxiliary storage (diskette) into main memory;
EDIT	make changes to the contents of a file in main memory (editing features are similar to those in the commercially available word processor WordStar);
FILE SAVE	save the contents of a file in main memory onto auxiliary storage (diskette);
RUN	compile and execute the machine code.

Files

Everything that resides on disk lives in a **file**. Each file must have its own **unique** file **name**. Rules for selecting file names are defined by DOS as follows:

    [d:]filename[.extension]

    [d:]   is an optional drive specifier:

        allowed drives are A, B, or C.

        If the drive is not specified, then DOS will assume the file is on the currently logged drive as indicated by the DOS A> B> or C> prompt.

filename	may be 1 to 8 characters in length,
	alphanumeric characters only.
	Do not use special characters or spaces as part of a file name.
extension	is optional, and may be 1 to 3 alphanumeric characters.

Conventions

Although DOS will allow you to select any filename you desire, it is wise to follow some common conventions. Pick names that allow you to easily identify the contents of a file. Because files may contain programs written in source code, executable object code, data to be used by programs, or even DOS commands, it is wise to include an extension to the file name to indicate the type of file that it is. Commonly used extensions are as follows:

.BAS	programs written in Basic source code
.DAT	files containing data to be used by programs
.EXE	executable object code
.COM	command files

Sample file names: (NOTE: upper and lower case are interchangeable)

          B:ASSIGN1.BAS   B:ASSIGN1.DAT

          A:COMMAND.COM   ACCOUNT.EXE

          WIDGET

Elements of Programming

A computer is capable of performing only a limited number of simple tasks. By combining these simple tasks in many different ways, we can achieve sophisticated results. Basically a computer can perform:

1. Input   bring data into memory from a data file or the keyboard.

2. Output   generate output to the screen, printer, or disk file.

3. Calculations perform arithmetic calculations.

4. Logic   perform logical decisions by means of comparing values.

5. Looping   repeating a sequence of operations until a condition exits.

When programming, you must remember that computers are essentially stupid. It is you, the programmer, who instructs the computer what to do by giving it a series of instructions in the form of a program. If you remember the following rules of programming, you will be well on your way to becoming an accomplished programmer:

- If you want the computer to do a particular thing, you must tell it in exacting detail to do that particular thing.

- If you don't tell it, it won't do it.

- The computer will do what you tell it to do, even if you didn't mean it to.

We all know the English language. We recognize that certain words indicate certain actions (i.e. run, walk, read, write). The Basic language is just another language. You must learn the words (instructions), and the syntax (punctuation and grammar), and then combine them in the proper order to produce the desired results.

Solving a Simple Problem Using BASIC

Statement of Problem: A Sports Store Inventory:

Suppose that you work for a company that sells sporting goods. Your task is to create a costed inventory report. The total stock value for each inventory item should be calculated as quantity on hand multiplied by item cost.

Input:

The company has a micro computer that they are currently using. They have a disk containing a data file of all their inventory items. They have many inventory items, and for each item the following data is kept:

> Item name, quantity on hand, unit cost

Output:

A report containing, for each inventory item, its name, the quantity on hand, the cost of the item, and the stock value for that item.

Even if you are very familiar with a programming language, you should resist the urge to code the program immediately. A simple stepwise approach it best to ensure that you fully understand the problem, and have all the tools (data and rules) to complete the task. This is a relatively simple problem and the solution may be clear immediately, but the more complicated programs make this stepwise logical process a must. The more time you spend on the initial design stage, the quicker and easier the programming will be.

Steps to Writing a Computer Program:

1. Define the desired results. Examine the problem carefully to decide exactly what output is required, and the most beneficial way to present it. This would include designing the report layout, and any totals and other summarization necessary in more complicated problems.

2. Ensure that the data provided from input are adequate to produce the desired results. If the input that is needed is not given, or is not in the correct form, you cannot proceed to the next step. Ask yourself "Can I use the data provided to calculate the required results using pen, paper, and a calculator?".

3. Develop an algorithm, or overall plan. An algorithm is a sequence of effective statements that, when applied to a problem, will solve it. Several of the most common techniques for designing an algorithm are flowcharts and pseudocode. These techniques are independent of the actual programming language used. They simply allow the programmer to express in general terms, in a *stepwise manner*, the actions that must be performed to achieve the desired output from the given input.

4. Write the code for the program. This involves translating the actions in the algorithm designed in the previous step into actual code, which in this case is QBASIC Code.

5. Enter the QBASIC code into the computer, and save the program under the desired file name.

6. Run the program. This involves compiling and executing the program. Using QBASIC, this step may be done by selecting the RUN option from the menu.

7. Test the results. There are two types of errors that may occur. Syntax errors are errors in the use of the Basic language. They will be indicated at compile time, and must be corrected before the program will execute. Logic errors are often more difficult to notice and correct. These are errors in your program logic. The program may execute, but not generate the desired results (i.e. perhaps you multiplied by 8 instead of .08 to calculate an 8% tax amount). Always check your output carefully to ensure that program produced the correct solutions in all cases. If either type of error exists, fix the code and repeat steps 6 and 7.

Applying the Stepwise Approach to the Sports Store Inventory Problem

Step 1.   **Define the results.**

The output for this problem should be in the following format. This is just a small excerpt of the report; the actual output would be a larger report.

Step 2.

| Hockey Stick | 23 | 18.75 | 431.25 |
| Badminton Net | 11 | 5.75 | 63.25 |

***** End of Report *****

Examine the input.

For our purposes, data to be input will be provided in a data **file**. Data files exist separately from the program. In order to write the program, the user must know exactly the format and order of the data that are to be input. A small portion of the data file to be used in this program is shown below.

A data file consists of a set of related data records. In this case the records are inventory records. Two records are shown above.

> Hockey Stick, 23, 18.75
>
> Badminton Net, 11, 5.75

The information in each record is divided into a number of fields. In this case each record contains 3 fields; item name, quantity on hand, and item cost.

Step 3.   **Designing the algorithm.**

Throughout this book we will use the **Top Down Design** approach to develop algorithms to solve problems. The concept of top down design is to look at the problem in an overview sense first, trying to avoid getting stuck on the details. The first step is to identify *what* you must do to solve the problem, not how you will do it. Once you have identified the major steps in the solution, you can then concentrate on the sub-steps of the the major steps.

The problem is continually divided into smaller and smaller sub-tasks. Tasks identified at each stage of this process are called **routines** or **modules**.

Any problem can be subdivided into at least four tasks or routines:

Mainline the controlling task, which dictates the order in which, and the number of times, the next three tasks are completed.

Initialization work to be performed at the start.

Process doing the work.

Termination the "clean up" work at the end.

In more complex problems, the Process task may be subdivided into even more sub-tasks.

A VTOC (Visual Table Of Contents) is used to show how all of the routines are related to each other. In this simplest case of just the four main routines, it is the Mainline routine that activates the other three routines. The VTOC would appear as follows:

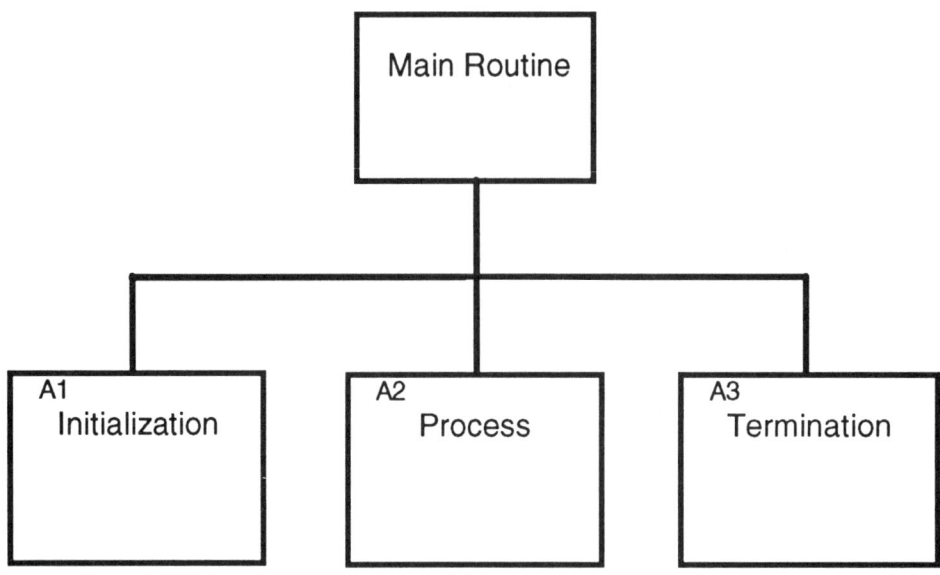

The next process in the Design step is to expand on each of the tasks (routines). Pseudocode or flowcharts are common methods for expressing each of the actions to be performed in a routine. Pseudocode is similar to real code, but very general in nature. It is not language specific, meaning that a programmer could work from the design created in pseudocode to code in any language (i.e. Basic, Cobol, etc.). The following is the pseudocode for the Sports Store inventory problem.

Mainline:

    Perform Initialization Routine

    Perform the Process Routine repeatedly until there are no more data records

    Perform the Termination Routine

Initialization:

    Open the data file

Process:

    Read data record

    Compute stock value = item cost x quantity on hand

    Print results

Termination:

    Print termination message

Let's examine each of the routines (tasks) in more detail:

The **Mainline** routine is responsible for directing the flow or order of execution of each of the other tasks. Obviously the initialization routine should be done first. Next the Process routine is repeated for every data record in the file. When all data records have been processed, the termination routine is done as a last and final step.

The **Initialization** routine is simple enough for this problem. It merely opens the data file for use. Opening is the task that instructs the computer to go to the disk, find the specified file, and prepare it for use.

The **Process** routine contains three actions to be performed. These actions will be performed for *every* data record in the file, because the mainline routine dictates that process routine should be *repeatedly* performed until there are no more data records to be read. The first action in the process routine is to read the next available data record from the disk into main memory. Recall that each data record contains three fields; item name, quantity on hand, and item cost. Once the data are in main memory, calculations can be performed to compute the stock value and store the calculated value in main memory. The last action is to print out the desired values from main memory. For this problem the desired output values are; item name, quantity on hand, item cost, and stock value.

The **Termination** routine is the final step in processing. It is always desirable to print some sort of message at the end of a report, indicating that it is indeed the end.

Step 4.   Write the code

This step involves turning each of the actions set out in the pseudocode from the previous step into actual Basic code. This will be done following **Structured Programming Techniques**. Structured programming techniques are formalized rules for coding programs. GOTOs are *not* allowed. Following the structured approach, any program can be written using the three basic constructs of:

    Sequence   successive statements executed in order; one entry point, one exit point.

    Selection   either of two operations to be carried out based on a condition.

    Looping   operation(s) to be repeated until a certain condition exists.

The code for the program is illustrated on the next page. It was generated based on the Design from step 3, following structured techniques. Each of the Basic statements used and the concept of a variable, input and output will be addressed in the next chapter.

```
' Program    : CH1EX1.BAS
' Programmer : John Scott
' Date       : June 4, 1990
' Data File  : CH1EX1.DAT
' Purpose    : To read records from the sports inventory file and
'            : print a report listing the value of the stock.
'
'Mainline
' ~~~~
    gosub init
    do until eof(1)
        gosub process
    loop
    gosub terminate
    end
' Init Routine
' ~~~~~
init:
    open "B:CH1EX1.DAT" for input as #1
    return
' Process Routine
' ~~~~~~~
process:
    input #1, item.name$, qty.on.hand, item.cost
    stock.value = qty.on.hand * item.cost
    print item.name$, qty.on.hand, item.cost, stock.value
    return
' Terminate Routine
' ~~~~~~~~
terminate:
    print
    print "***** End of Report *****"
    return
' End of Program File
' ~~~~~~~~~
```

Review Questions

1. What is the makeup of a valid file name in DOS?

2. List the seven steps in solving a computer problem.

3. List the four major routines in a structured program.

4. Which routine controls the execution of the other routines?

5. Draw the VTOC for a program containing the four major routines.

6. In which of the four major routines would you include the following actions?

    - Print the termination message.

    - Read a data record.

    - Open the data file.

    - Perform calculations based on the input from the data record.

    - Print out values from the data record and calculated values.

Chapter 1   Problem Solving   13

Programming Problem:

1. Using QBASIC, type in the program CH1EX1.BAS at the end of the chapter exactly as shown. Then type in the data file CH1EX1.DAT containing the three records worth of data exactly as show below. Be careful that the last line ends by pressing the Enter key. Do not include blank lines anywhere in the data file.

   Hockey Stick, 23, 18.75

   Badminton Net, 11, 5.75

   Baseball Bat, 13, 17.61

   Run the program. You may need to correct typing errors. Ultimately you should see three lines of output in the output window.

CHAPTER 2

BASIC Statements

BASIC Statements	**15**
REM Statement	**15**
GOSUB and RETURN Statements	**16**
OPEN Statement	**17**
The Concept of Variables	**18**
Variable Types	**19**
INPUT Statement	**20**
LET (Assignment) Statement	**21**
PRINT and LPRINT Statements	**22**
DO and LOOP Statements	**23**
END Statement	**24**
Summary	**24**
Review Questions	**26**

Basic Statements

Each Basic statement begins with a **keyword** that identifies the action to be performed. Seven Basic keywords, or types of statements, were used in the sports store inventory program in the previous chapter. Each keyword must be used in the proper context, with the appropriate syntax.

The statement may be typed in upper or lower case, as both are equivalent. The only exception to this is when data are in quotes. In this case, the text between quotes will be stored and/or printed exactly as it appears. It is, however, common practice to use lower case when entering code, and use upper case only for displaying titles, headings and text for program output. QBASIC automatically changes keywords to upper case.

The number of blank spaces at the start of a statement, or between the words in a statement does not affect how Basic interprets the statement. Common conventions dictate that all code (except labels and remarks) should begin several positions in from the leftmost character position, and should line up with the previous statements. Further indentation for conditional statements will be covered later. Spacing between the components of a statement should be such that the statement is "easy to read".

REM Statement (')

REM is short for REMARK. Remark statements are used to insert comment or descriptive lines of text into a program. A single quote may be used in place of the word REM, and is preferable as it makes the code easier to read.

Any statement beginning with the keyword REM or a single quote is ignored by Basic during the running of a program, but will still be printed or displayed with the listing of the program. Remarks may also be added at the end of other statements by inserting a single quote after the statement and before the remark.

Sample:

```
REM  this is a remark or comment line
rem  this is also a remark...case does not matter
' Likewise this is a remark line
let x = a * b    ' a remark at the end of a statement
```

Remarks are commonly used to describe the purpose of the program, when it was written and by whom, to clarify portions of the code that could be more easily understood by humans if some written explanation was given, and also to provide more attractive vertical spacing, just as a person writing a book might include blank lines between paragraphs.

Programming standards for this course require all programs to contain remarks at the start of the program indicating:

- the actual file name of the Basic program file on disk;

- the author's name;

- the date;

- the name of the data file on disk;

- a general program description.

Blank lines to improve the appearance and ease of reading a program listing should be inserted at the start and end of all subroutines. Either a completely blank line or a line beginning with a single quote is acceptable. Lines beginning with a single quote are actually better, as Basic can compile them faster than blank lines. Can you justify why this is so?

GOSUB and RETURN Statements

QBASIC will execute the instructions in a program, beginning at the first instruction and proceeding sequentially, executing each instruction in order. Our program, however, was designed following Top Down Design techniques. The total program consists of several distinct routines. The mainline routine must direct the execution to each of the other three routines in the correct order. This is accomplished through the use of a GOSUB statement and its companion statement RETURN.

Sample:
    GOSUB **label**

The GOSUB statement causes Basic to jump to the **label** found elsewhere in the program, and continue execution from that position. A RETURN statement must be coded at the end of a subroutine. When Basic executes the RETURN statement, execution will jump back to the statement after the GOSUB which sent it to that routine.

Sample:
>   RETURN

A label must appear on a line by itself (though a remark may follow). Labels must begin with a letter, and can contain any number of letters and digits. The label must be followed by a colon; however the GOSUB label statement that refers to it must not have a colon after the label.

Basic does not limit the label names that you may choose, but choosing descriptive meaningful names makes a program easier to read and understand. Since label names are required for each routine in a program, standard names like: INIT, PROCESS, and TERMINATE are best as they are descriptive, and commonly used by programmers.

```
            .
            .
        gosub init
            .
            .
  init:
            .
            .
        return
```

OPEN Statement

Data files are stored separately from program files. Thus, there must be a link between the program file with the instructions and the data file to be used for that program. This is accomplished by an OPEN statement. A data file must be opened before any data may be accessed (read) from it.

Sample:
>   OPEN "B:ASSIGN1.DAT" FOR INPUT AS #1

The actual file name of the data file on disk must be provided in double quotes. Refer to the section on files in the previous chapter for valid file names.

Files may be opened for input, output or both. For the purposes of our programs files will be used only to provide data *to* the program, and are hence INPUT files.

The OPEN statement assigns a data file on disk, to an internal number (in the above case #1, although numbers 1, 2 and 3 are valid). Whenever the file is referenced in the program, the internal file number assigned in the OPEN statement is used, as opposed to the actual file name on disk. This will be explained in more detail when the INPUT statement is covered.

When Basic executes the OPEN statement, it will search the disk for the specified file. If it is not found an error message will be generated, and execution will stop. If the file is successfully located on disk, it will be "opened" and the data contained in the file will be available to be read later by an INPUT statement.

The Concept of Variables

The term "variable" is given to a spot in memory that can contain a numeric or character (string) value. Recall that computer programs can only perform operations on values that are in main memory, not auxiliary memory such as disk. A variable in Basic is much like a variable in algebra. It is a symbol or name that is used to represent a value that can change (i.e. in converting Farenheit to Celsius   C = (F - 32) * 5 / 9 the symbol F is used to represent farenheit value, and C to represent Celsius).

You cannot take the cover off a computer and actually see the contents of main memory, but perhaps it would help to visualize it as a large storage area, much like a series of post office boxes. There would be an area of main memory where DOS is stored, another where the QBASIC compiler is stored, another where the object code of the currently executing program is stored, and another for variables used by the currently executing program.

When a variable is first referenced in a program, a spot in memory is reserved by that variable name. For the rest of the time that the program is executing, this memory spot can always be found by referring to it by its variable name.

Chapter 2 BASIC Statements 19

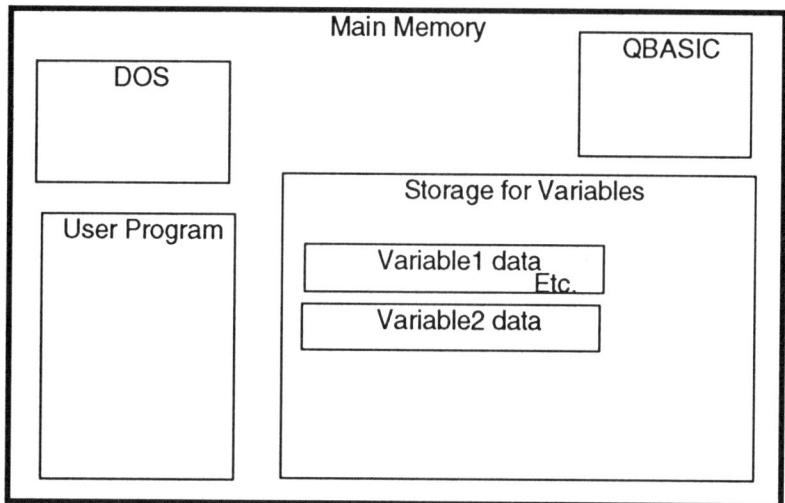

There are rules for selecting valid names for variables:

- must start with a character;

- can contain up to 40 letters, digits or periods (.);

- may not be a reserved word (see appendix 1);

- may not begin with the letters FN.

Always pick meaningful variable names. Someone reading your program for the first time should be able to easily understand what a variable contains, based upon the name you gave it. Periods provide a nice way of "punctuating" variable names so they are easier to read. For example although QBASIC would not complain about a variable called IC, a better choice would be ITEM.COST as it clearly indicates what the variable contains. Case does not matter (i.e. **ITEM.COST** and **item.cost** are the same variable).

Variable Types

There are two main types of variables; NUMERIC and STRING.

NUMERIC variables can only contain pure numbers. A pure number consists only of digits, one decimal point, and a plus or minus sign. Commas for thousands, dollar signs, percent signs, etc. are symbols *not* allowed in a numeric variable memory spot.

STRING variables can contain absolutely any character. A string variable is differentiated from a numeric variable by including a $ (dollar sign) as the last character of the variable name. This dollar sign simply indicates the variable as string type, and has no relationship to dollar amounts. String variables typically contain alpha-type data such as name, address, phone numbers, social insurance numbers, etc.

Some data fields seem to border the division between numeric and string. Data such as part number, customer number, student number could be contained in either a numeric or a string variable. The best approach is if the information is to be used for arithmetic, it must be stored as numeric, but if the information is only for identification, then it is best stored as string.

Valid Variable Names	**Invalid Variable Names**
stock.price	price-of-item (dashes not allowed)
item.name$	name$ (reserved word)
first.cost	1st.cost (starts with digit)
namee$	FNAME (starts with FN)
F.NAME$	

At the start of execution of a QBASIC program, all numeric variables contain the value 0 (zero), and string variables contain nothing (null). Consequently when a programmer misspells a variable name in a program, the computer tries to a find that variable in memory by the misspelled name and treats it as if it was found and contained the value 0 or null.

There are two ways to store data into variables;

- INPUT the data into the variables.

- assign (LET) the values to the variable.

INPUT Statement

The purpose of the INPUT statement is to bring data from a data file into variable locations in main memory. Recall that this is necessary because a computer can only work on data stored in main memory.

Suppose our inventory file had 25 records of data. This is to say there are 25 different sports items for which there is information in the data file. For each record there are three fields of data: item name, quantity on hand, item cost. In total there would be 75 (25 x 3) entries in the data file. Would this mean that we would need 75 different variables? NO. There are only three variables required to hold the data from the file: one for each field (item name, quantity on hand, item cost). The program processes the data in the file **one** record at at time. The data for a record are input, then all processing for this data is completed. Thus the same variables can be **re-used** for the data from the next record when they are input and processed.

An INPUT statement is used to "pull" data from a designated data file into variables.

SAMPLE:
    INPUT #1, ITEM.NAME$, QTY.ON.HAND, ITEM.COST

The #1 in the statement is the internal file reference number. This must be the same number used in the OPEN statement. Note that a comma follows the file number, and separates each variable name.

When the above statement is executed, the next three pieces of data will be copied from the data file and stored in the three variables respectively in main memory. The first piece of data may contain non-numeric data because of the $ indicating it is a string variable. The next two pieces of data must be pure numeric data, or the program will complain with a TYPE MISMATCH error and execution will stop.

LET (Assignment) Statement

The other method to store values into variables is by using an assignment statement know as the LET statement.

Sample:
    LET STOCK.VALUE = QTY.ON.HAND * ITEM.COST

The portion of the statement to the right of the equal sign is the expression. An expression can be composed of variables or constants (actual numbers) separated by arithmetic operators. The five common operator symbols are:

+ addition
- subtraction
* multiplication
/ division
^ raising to a power

The hierarchy of operations in QBASIC follows normal arithmetic rules:

- expressions in brackets evaluated first;
- multiplication and division next;
- addition and subtraction.

When the LET statement is executed, the expression is evaluated by obtaining the values from the variables in main memory, and performing the operations indicated to calculate the result. The result (answer) is then stored in the variable to the left of the equal sign.

The LET statement can be written with or without the the keyword LET. It is most commonly written *without* the keyword LET.

```
STOCK.VALUE = QTY.ON.HAND * ITEM.COST
```

Constants (actual numeric amounts) can be used directly in assignment statements. In the following statement, the tax rate is coded as a constant.

```
TAX = SALE.AMOUNT * .08
```

PRINT and LPRINT Statements

Most computer programs require that some sort of output be generated so the user may see the result of processing. Output from the execution of a program may be sent to the computer monitor (screen) or the printer. The keyword PRINT will cause information from the memory of the machine to be sent to the monitor, whereas the keyword LPRINT will direct the output to the printer.

The simplest form of the PRINT statement is the keyword PRINT followed by a list of items to print, separated by commas, semicolons or spaces. The use of a comma, semicolon or space affects where the output will be positioned on the screen or paper.

comma   the item following the comma will be placed in the next available print zone. Print zones are every 14 positions and may be thought of like typewriter tabs at positions 1, 15, 29, etc. The use of commas provides for quick and tidy output in a columnar fashion.

semicolon or   causes each item to be printed next to the previous one,
space   ignoring print zones.

The list of items to print can include variables, constants, expressions, and literals. A literal is a phrase in quotes. When a variable is included in the print list, the computer retrieves the current value stored in the variable in main memory and prints that value.

Sample:
    PRINT ITEM.NAME$, QTY.ON.HAND, ITEM.COST, STOCK.VALUE

causes the current value of the four variables to be printed in columns on the screen

    PRINT "EMPLOYEE WITH BONUS";EMP.NAME$

causes the phrase EMPLOYEE WITH BONUS to be printed, directly followed by the current contents of the variable EMP.NAME$.

BASIC distinguishes a variable from a phrase by the fact that variable names are **not** in quotes. If the programmer forgot to include quotes around the phrase EMPLOYEE WITH BONUS, Basic would print the contents of three numeric variables; EMPLOYEE, WITH, and BONUS. Likely there would be no variables by those names in main memory, causing Basic to print each as if they contained the value 0. Output from the erroneous statement may appear as;

0   0   0   Sue Smith

When the programmer expected to see;

EMPLOYEE WITH BONUS   Sue Smith

DO and LOOP Statement

DO and LOOP are a pair of statements used to cause the **repetition** of a sequence of statements until a particular condition arises. There are many variations of the DO statement. Only a simple example will be covered at this point.

In a structured program, the most common use of a DO LOOP is to repeat the execution of the PROCESS routine *until* all the data records have been input (i.e., the end of the data file is reached). The condition for ending the loop is included in the DO statement. All statements between the DO statement and the LOOP statement will be executed UNTIL the condition becomes true. It is good form to *indent* all statements between the DO and LOOP statement to indicate that they are only executed depending on the condition.

Sample:

```
DO UNTIL EOF(1)
    PERFORM PROCESS
LOOP
```

EOF(1) must be coded as shown. EOF stands for End Of File. The number in brackets corresponds to the internal file number as assigned in the OPEN statement for the data file. The EOF condition is recognized when the last piece of data is read from the file.

END Statement

Sample:

```
END
```

The END statement is simple in form, but the placement of it is critical in a structured program. When QBASIC executes the END statement the execution of the program is stopped. In a structured program, the END statement must be placed at the end of the MAINLINE routine. Without the END statement, QBASIC would continue to execute the next sequential statement after the end of the MAINLINE routine. In most programs, this would be the first statement in the INIT routine. This logic error is known as "falling through" the code, because the initialization routine should not be executed again at this time.

SUMMARY

The best way to fully understand the Basic statements, and the concepts of a variable, a data file and program execution introduced in this chapter is to **walk through** the sample Stock Inventory program code, pretending that you are the computer. Prepare for this exercise by having a listing of the data file, a listing of the program code, and two pieces of paper. One piece of paper is to be treated as if it was the output screen (or printer), the other as if it was main memory. On the "memory page" draw and name a box for each variable as it is used in the program. Begin by pretending to execute each statement in the same order as QBASIC would. If the statement affects the contents of a variable in memory, erase the current value for the variable and insert the new value on your "memory page." If the statement causes output, then write the results on your "output page."

This walk-through technique is also used to debug (find the logic errors in) a program that has problems. It becomes much clearer what your program is actually doing when you can follow and identify the actions yourself on paper.

Review Questions

1. What is the statement used to place comments within a Basic program? What are two ways of coding this statement?

2. Identify which of the following are invalid variable names and why they are invalid.

    NAME
    fname
    flrSt-NAme
    student.name$
    student.number$
    1st.name
    soc.in num
    $first
    LEN
    nam $
    nam$

3. What is the purpose of the GOSUB and RETURN statements?

4. Write the Basic statement to open a file called EMPLOY.DAT on drive B for input as file 1.

5. Write the Basic statement to read in data from the above data file, given that each record contains employee number, date of birth, and gross pay to date. Make up your own variable names.

6. How many times would the INIT routine be executed in a program run?

7. In which routine would you include the following actions?

    Open the data file
    Perform calculations based on the data record input
    Print the ending message
    Perform the Process routine
    Read a data record

8. Which statement(s) cause the Process routine to be executed more than once?

9. How many times would the process routine be executed in a program?

10. What would be the output from the following statements provided that the variable NAM$ contained "SUSAN" and the variable MARKS contained 88?

    PRINT "NAM$, received , marks"
    print NAM$,"received", marks
    print nam$;marks

11. Identify (circle and correct) the errors in the following program:

    .'Program   :errors.bas
    'Programmer   :Not so Hot
    'Data File   :invent.dat
    'Date   :Sept. 19/90
    '
    '
    'Mainline
    '~~~~~~~~
    gosub init
    do until eof(2)
        gosub process
        loop
        gosub terminate
    'Initialization routine
    '~~~~~~~~~~~~~~~~~~~~~~
    initial:
        open invent.dat for input as 1
        return
    'Process routine
    '~~~~~~~~~~~~~~~~
    process:
        input product.name, opening.bal, received, sold, cost
        closing.bal = opening.bal - received + sold
        value = closing.bal * cost
        print product.name, opening.bal, closing, value
    'Terminatation routine
    '~~~~~~~~~~~~~~~~~~~~~
    'terminate:
        lprint
        lprint "********* end of processing ************"
        return

Programming Problems

Problem #1 - Net Pay Report

INSTRUCTIONS:

A report is to be prepared that calculates employees net pay based on gross pay and deductions. A program should be designed and coded in BASIC to produce the report.

INPUT:

Input consists of records that contain employee ID, gross pay, CPP deduction, and UI deduction. Build a data file that includes the following data. Make sure to include a comma to separate data items. No comma is required at the end of a line. Be sure that your data file does not contain extra blank lines at the end.

```
L143, 542.32, 153.21, 56.32
S232, 332.41, 0, 62.31
T832, 794.62, 54.28, 123.76
T932, 66.32, 0, 0
W153, 643.40, 77.92, 44.56
```

OUTPUT:

Calculate net pay as gross pay minus CPP and UI deductions. Print out a report containing one line for each employee showing employee ID and net pay.

Challenge Adaptations:

i) Print out the total deductions between the employee ID and net pay fields.

ii) Include column headings on the report.

iii) Print out a count of the number of employees in the data file at the end of the report.

Problem #2 - Pay Calculation

INSTRUCTIONS:

A report is to be prepared that calculates an employees weekly gross pay given hours worked and rate of pay. A program should be designed and coded in BASIC to produce the report.

INPUT:

Input consists of records that contain employee name, hours worked and pay rate per hour. Build a data file that includes the following data. Make sure to include a comma to separate data items. No comma is required at the end of a line. Be sure that your data file does not contain extra blank lines at the end.

> John Doe, 33, 10.60
> Kevin Smith, 20, 5.96
> Jane Bartley, 48, 15.63
> Bev Minnis, 13, 7.83

OUTPUT:

Calculate net gross pay as hours worked times rate per hour. Print out a report containing one line for each employee, showing name, hours worked and gross pay.

Challenge Adaptations:

i) Include column headings on the report.

ii) Print out total gross pay at the end of the report.

CHAPTER 3

Headings and Totals

Headings and Totals	**31**
Headings	**31**
Counts and Totals	**33**
Flowcharting	**38**
Review Questions	**41**

Headings and Totals

The program developed in the previous chapter produced output that contained four columns of data; item name, quantity on hand, item cost and stock value. While this report contained the necessary data, it could be improved by printing headings at the top of the report, and printing a count of the number of items and total stock value at the end as shown below. The headings serve the purpose of identifying what information is presented in each column. The count and total are useful to the user of the report to identify the number of inventory items, and the total stock value.

SPORTS EMPORIUM STOCK REPORT

Item Name	Qty. On Hand	Item Cost	Stock Value
Hockey Stick	23	18.75	431.25
Badminton Net	11	5.75	63.25

Number of Items   : 2
Total Stock Value : 494.5

***** End of Report *****

Headings

Headings are displayed at the start of the program output. Typically the first heading line(s) contain a report title and company name. Subsequent heading line(s) contain column headings to describe the columns of output.

The pseudocode developed for the program in the previous chapter can be enhanced to include the output of report headings. In which of the four routines (MAINLINE, INIT, PROCESS, or TERMINATE) would you include the action to output the headings? Think about the purpose of each of the routines, and the order they are executed in to determine the correct placement. The MAINLINE routine is used to direct the flow of execution, and should be left as just a controlling routine. The INIT routine contains actions that are done one time only, before the processing of the data is done.

Next, the PROCESS routine contains actions to be be repeated many times, once for each data record in the data file. Finally the TERMINATION routine contains actions that are done one time only, after all other processing is done.

Since headings are to be output at the start of the report (before the data is processed) it would only be logical to place this action in the INIT routine. The pseudocode for the INIT would be enhanced by adding the highlighted action:

INITIALIZATION:

> Open the data file
>
> Print Report Headings

Note: it does not matter whether the headings are printed before or after the data file is opened in the INIT routine.

Pseudocode is very general, which is why a simple action like "print report headings" is all that is necessary. The programmer will have to translate this action to the statements necessary to complete the task when programming the problem. What statements should the programmer code to cause the headings to be printed?

The first question a new programmer should ask is "What Basic keyword causes output to be generated?" The only statement that causes output is the PRINT (or LPRINT) statement. The second question is "What is it I want to print in the headings?" Looking back at the sample output we can see that there are really four heading lines; a title, a blank line, column headings, and another blank line. This would translate to four PRINT statements as follows:

```
PRINT "          SPORTS EMPORIUM STOCK REPORT"
PRINT
PRINT "Item Name", "Qty. On Hand", "Item Cost", "Stock Value"
PRINT
```

The values to be printed are in quotes so that the actual string of characters is printed. Remember that if quotes were not used, Basic would interpret the words as variable names, and attempt to print the contents of those variables. Spaces are included in the quotes in the first print statement to effectively centre the title on the page. Only what is in the quotes will be printed, spaces outside of the quotes have no affect on the spacing of the output.

A PRINT statement with nothing after it causes a blank line to be printed.

Column headings are printed in each print zone by separating them with commas. Note that the comma is not inside the quotes as this would cause a comma to be printed in the heading rather than causing the action of skipping to the next print zone.

Counts and Totals

Most problems require that a summary of the data processed be printed at the end of the report. In the case of the sports store inventory, the summary should include a count of the number of items and a total of the inventory stock value.

Producing final counts and totals in a computer program requires the same actions that you would do manually if using a calculator. The difference is that **variables** would be used in a computer program, rather than a calculator. When variables are used for calculating the count of something or accumulating the total of something, we refer to these variables as Counters and Accumulators. They are still just variables, but their names identify what the variables are being used for.

Three distinct actions are involved in counting and accumulating:

- initializing the counters and accumulators to zero at the beginning of processing (similar to clearing a calculator at the start);

- incrementing the counters and accumulators for each record of data processed;

- displaying the final value of the counter and accumulator at the end.

First the pseudocode should be modified to include the necessary actions for producing totals. Approach this in the same manner as the headings were handled, by asking yourself "In which modules would I include the above actions?"

Variables for the counter and accumulator would be initialized to zero at the start of the processing, and therefore in the INIT routine.

The counter should be increased by 1 and the accumulator should be increased by the stock value each time a record is processed. Since the individual records are processed in the PROCESS routine, the counting and accumulating actions must be done there.

The final value stored in the counter and accumulator should be printed at the end of the report. This would therefore be done in the TERMINATION routine.

The enhancements for counters and totals, and printing headings are highlighted in the following pseudocode:

Mainline:

    Perform Initialization Routine

    Perform the Process Routine repeatedly until there are no more data records

    Perform the Termination Routine

Initialization:

    Open the data file

    <mark>Initialize counter and total to 0</mark>
    <mark>Print Report Headings</mark>

Process:

    Read data record

    Compute stock value = unit cost x quantity on hand

    <mark>Increase count by 1</mark>
    <mark>Increase total stock value by stock value</mark>

    Print results

Termination:

    <mark>Print count and total stock value</mark>

    Print termination message

Now that the actions, and placement of the actions have been included in the program design for counters and accumulators, the actual Basic coding may be examined.

First the programmer must select variable names for the counter and accumulator variables. ITEM.COUNT and TOTAL.STOCK.VALUE are acceptable names as they clearly indicate the variables' purposes.

Initializing the counter and accumulator variables to zero is accomplished by a LET statement. Recall that the keyword LET is optional, and usually not used. Thus the statements to store the value 0 into the variables would be:

```
ITEM.COUNT = 0
TOTAL.STOCK.VALUE = 0
```

The statements to increase the contents of counters and accumulators are placed in the PROCESS routine. Counters are incremented by adding the value of 1 to the current value in the counter variable, and storing this new value back into the counter variable. This is done using the LET statement. Recall that when the LET statement is executed, the expression on the right of the equal sign is evaluated, and the result (answer) is stored in the variable on the left of the equal sign. Totals are accumulated in the same manner. The only difference is that instead of adding 1, the amount you wish to accumulate is added.

```
ITEM.COUNT = ITEM.COUNT + 1
TOTAL.STOCK.VALUE = TOTAL.STOCK.VALUE + STOCK.VALUE
```

Let's examine how the counter variable ITEM.COUNT is incremented. It was initialized to 0 in the INIT routine. During the first pass through the PROCESS routine the expression ITEM.COUNT + 1 will be evaluated as 0 + 1. The result (i.e., 1) will be stored back in the variable ITEM.COUNT. During the second pass through the process routine the expression will be evaluated as 1 + 1, and the result (i.e., 2) will be stored back in ITEM.COUNT. This action is repeated for each pass through the PROCESS routine (data record processed), therefore after the last record has been processed, the value left in the variable ITEM.COUNT will be equal to the number of data records processed.

Accumulators are handled similarly. In this case the variable TOTAL.STOCK.VALUE would have been initialized to 0 in the INIT routine. During the first pass through the process routine the expression TOTAL.STOCK.VALUE + STOCK.VALUE would be evaluated as 0 + the calculated value stored in STOCK.VALUE (i.e., 0 + 431.25). The result (i.e.,

431.25) would be stored back in the variable TOTAL.STOCK.VALUE. During the second pass through the process routine the expression would be evaluated as 431.25 + 63.25 and the result (i.e. 494.5) would be stored back in the variable TOTAL.STOCK.VALUE. After the last record has been processed, the variable TOTAL.STOCK.VALUE will contain the final sum of the all of the stock values for the individual data records.

By the time the TERMINATE routine is executed, all data records will have been processed, thus the count and total variable will contain the final values. The output for this program displays a blank line before the summary, and a phrase describing the count and total before the values to clearly indicate what they are. The PRINT statements to accomplish this would be:

```
PRINT
PRINT "NUMBER OF ITEMS :";ITEM.COUNT
PRINT "TOTAL STOCK VALUE:";TOTAL.STOCK.VALUE
```

The original Basic program has been enhanced to include all the statements required to produce headings and summary totals. The added statements are highlighted in the code on the following page.

```
' Program    : CH3EX1.BAS
' Programmer : John Scott
' Date       : June 6, 1990
' Data File  : CH3EX1.DAT
' Purpose    : To read records from the sports inventory
'            : file and print a report listing the value of
'            : the stock Report has column headings and
'            : report totals
' Mainline
' ~~~~
  gosub init
  do until eof(1)
    gosub process
  loop
  gosub terminate
  end
' Init Routine
' ~~~~~
init:
  open "A:CH3EX1.DAT" for input as #1
  print
  print "          SPORTS EMPORIUM STOCK REPORT"
  print
  print "Item Name","Qty. On Hand","Item Cost","Stock Value"
  print
  item.count = 0
  total.stock.value = 0
  return
' Process Routine
' ~~~~~~~~
process:
  input #1, item.name$, qty.on.hand, item.cost
  stock.value = qty.on.hand * item.cost
  print item.name$, qty.on.hand, item.cost, stock.value
  item.count = item.count + 1
  total.stock.value = total.stock.value + stock.value
  return

' Terminate Routine
' ~~~~~~~~
terminate:
  print
  print "Number of Items    :"; item.count
  print "Total Stock Value  :"; total.stock.value
  print
  print "***** End of Report *****"
  return
' End of Program File
' ~~~~~~~~~
```

Flowcharting

Another way of expressing program design, besides pseudocode, is flowcharting. Both flowcharts and pseudocode serve the same purpose. It is up to the individual, the instructor, or the company, to select the method preferred.

Flowcharting is pictoral, and often beginner programmers find it easier to conceptualize than pseudocode. Flowcharts use a limited set of **symbols** to represent actions. The symbols are connected by flow lines to indicate the direction of flow.

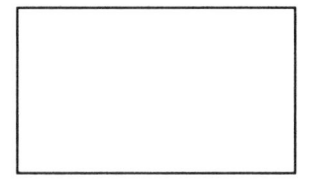

- the processing symbol used to express actions that contain actual information processing operations (usually equate to assignment actions and arithmetic operations in Basic)

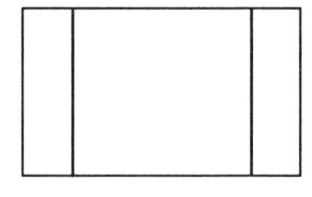

- the predefined process symbol is used to represent the execution of a routine described in more detail elsewhere in the flowchart

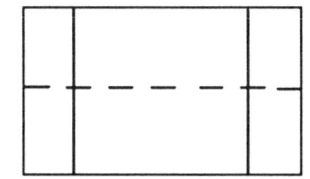

- the repetitive predefined process symbol is used to represent the execution of a routine until a certain condition occurs

- the input/output symbol represents any input or output action

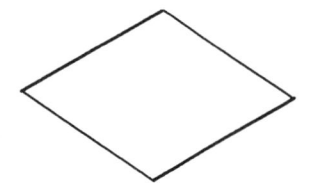

- the decision symbol is used to represent where a logical decision is made and one of two courses of action are taken depending on the result of the decision

- the termination symbol represents the start or end of a program or routine

- the connector symbol is used to connect the end of a flow in one physical stop to the continuing section of the same flow elsewhere

The flowchart for the enhanced program with headings and summary totals would be as follows:

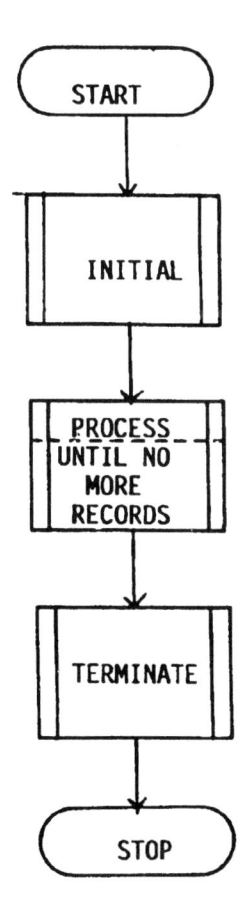

```
         ┌─────────┐
         │  START  │
         └────┬────┘
              ▼
         ┌─────────┐
         │ INITIAL │
         └────┬────┘
              ▼
         ┌─────────┐
         │ PROCESS │
         │UNTIL NO │
         │  MORE   │
         │ RECORDS │
         └────┬────┘
              ▼
         ┌─────────┐
         │TERMINATE│
         └────┬────┘
              ▼
         ┌─────────┐
         │  STOP   │
         └─────────┘
```

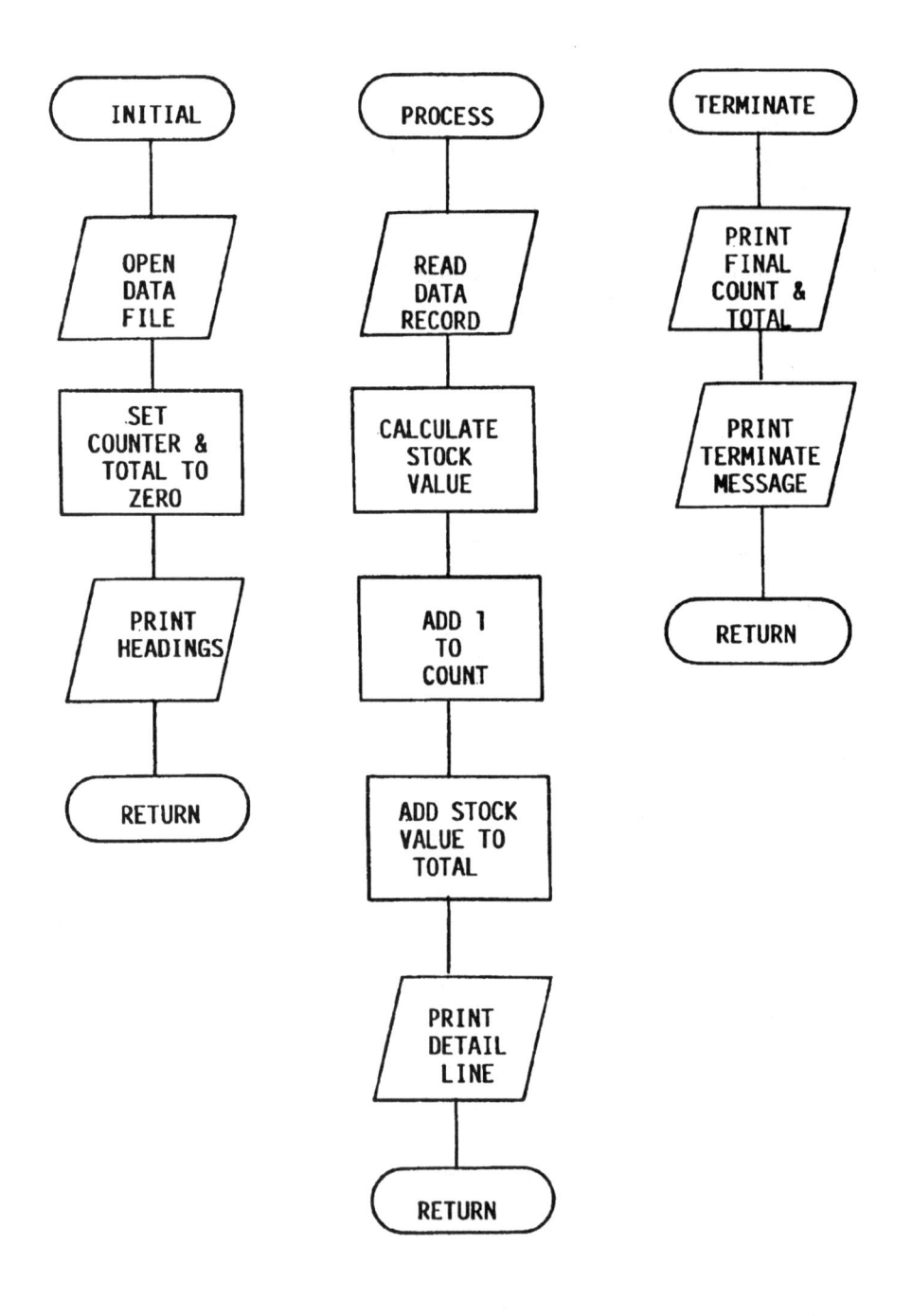

```
   INITIAL              PROCESS             TERMINATE
      |                    |                    |
   OPEN                 READ                 PRINT
   DATA                 DATA                 FINAL
   FILE                 RECORD               COUNT &
      |                    |                 TOTAL
   SET                  CALCULATE              |
   COUNTER &            STOCK                PRINT
   TOTAL TO             VALUE                TERMINATE
   ZERO                    |                 MESSAGE
      |                 ADD 1                  |
   PRINT                TO                   RETURN
   HEADINGS             COUNT
      |                    |
   RETURN               ADD STOCK
                        VALUE TO
                        TOTAL
                           |
                        PRINT
                        DETAIL
                        LINE
                           |
                        RETURN
```

Review Questions

1. In which routine would you include the following actions?

    Increment the count of the number of records processed.

    Print report title.

    Print column headings.

    Print the count of the number of records processed.

    Accumulate (add up) a final total of amounts calculated.

2. Which of the following statements could not be used to accumulate running totals or counts?

    Count = 1

    total.fees = total.fees + 1

    number.records = number.records + number.records

    count = count + 1

    total = total.fees + fees

    total = fees + total

3. Use the "desk trace" method of stepping through the execution of the program on the following page. Use the data file shown below.

i) Show the output.

ii) Identify all corrections necessary to make the program work logically.

   Data File Contents:
   Widget, 15.00
   Gadget, 28.00
   Ringer, 7.50
   Balaster, 10.10

Program for Review Question 3:

```
'mainline
gosub init
do until eof(1)
    gosub process
loop
gosub terminate
end
init:
    open "inventry.dat" for input as #1
    lprint ,"INVENTORY MARKUP REPORT"
    lprint
    return
process:
    lprint "PRODUCT","COST","20% MARKUP","PRICE"
    input #1,product$,price
    markup = cost * 20
    price = cost + markup
    lprint product$, cost, markup, price
    count = count + 1
    return
terminate:
    lprint
    lprint "Number of Stutents: ";count
    total.price = total.price + price
    lprint "Total Price", total.price
    return
```

Programming Problems:

Problem #1 - Student Averages

INSTRUCTIONS:

A report is to be prepared that calculates students' averages based on test scores. A program should be designed and coded in BASIC to produce the report.

INPUT:

Input consists of records that contain students' names, followed by their marks for four different tests. Build a data file that includes the following data. Make sure to include a comma to separate data items. No comma is required at the end of a line. Be sure that your data file does not contain extra blank lines at the end of it.

```
Susan Brown     64  72   57 86
Doug Claver     98  61   82 86
Jim Richard     82  85   72 78
Maria Smith     91  82   61 70
Stephen White   49  62   75 81
```

OUTPUT:

Calculate the total points earned as the sum of the marks for the first three tests, plus twice the final exam mark. Then calculate the average by dividing the total points earned by 5.

Print out a report with appropriate headings. The report is to contain student name, total points earned, and average, plus a summary at the end.

The output should appear as follows:

Class Standings

Student Name	Total Points Earned	Average
Susan Brown	365	73
Doug Claver	413	82.6
Jim Richard	395	79
Maria Smith	374	74.8
Stephen White	348	69.6

Number of Stutents: 5
Class Average   : 75.8

Problem #2 - Transportation Charges

INSTRUCTIONS:

A report is to be prepared for the cost of transporting landscaping products for a nursery. A program should be designed and coded in BASIC to produce the report.

INPUT:

Input consists of records that contain a product number, the product name, the length, width, and height of the container that contains the product, the weight per cubic foot, and transportation charges per pound for each product. Build a sequential data file containing the following data.

PRODUCT NUMBER	PRODUCT NAME	LENGTH (FEET)	WIDTH (FEET)	HEIGHT (FEET)	WEIGHT PER CUBIC FOOT	TRANS. COST PER LB.
15	BRICK	2	3	3	126	.01
22	CORK	4	4	4	16	.08
45	SOIL	3	3	2	69	.02
67	SAND	2	2	3	91	.02

Chapter 3 Headings and Totals 45

OUTPUT:

Output is a report of transportation charges. The report is to contain the product name, the number of cubic feet (obtained by multiplying the length times the width times the height), the total weight (obtained by multiplying the number of cubic feet by the weight per cubic foot), and the total transportation charges (obtained by multiplying the total weight by the transportation cost per pound). After all records have been processed, the total records processed, the total cubic feet, the total weight, and the total transportation charges are to be printed in a summary report. The format of the output is illustrated below.

Transportation Charges

Product Name	Cubic Feet	Total Weight	Transportation Charges
BRICK	18	2268	22.68
CORK	64	1024	81.92
SOIL	18	1242	24.84
SAND	12	1092	21.84

Number of Items: 4
Total Cubic Feet: 112
Total Weight: 5626
Total Transportation Charges: 151.28

Problem #3 - Rental Charges

INSTRUCTIONS:

A report of charges is to be prepared for a mobile hot tub rental company. A program should be designed and coded in BASIC to produce the report.

INPUT:

Input consists of records which contain a customer name, a customer number, the number of days the tub was rented, the rental charge per day for that tub, the charge for chemicals required, and the transportation charge for delivering and picking up the tub. Build a sequential data file containing the following data.

CUSTOMER NAME	CUSTOMER NUMBER	NO. OF DAYS	CHARGE/ DAY	CHEMICAL CHARGE	TRANSPORTATION CHARGE
MATHEWS	14	2	15.00	9.00	14.25
BLOOM	26	1	54.00	-	10.00
HUTTON	35	7	16.00	26.00	-
LEWIS	41	2	35.00	7.00	28.50

OUTPUT:

Output is a report of rental charges. The report is to contain customer name, taxable charge, non-taxable charge, and total customer charge including tax. Chemicals and rental charges are taxable at 8%. Rental charge is the number of days the tub is rented for, times the daily rental charge. Transportation charge is non-taxable. The total charge including tax is therefore the taxable charge + the 8% tax on that amount + the non-taxable charge. After all records have been processed, display a summary of totals. This must include the number of customers processed, the total rental charges, the total chemical charges, the total transportation charges, and the total of all charges including tax. The format of the output is illustrated below.

Rental Charges

Customer Name	Taxable Charge	Non-Taxable Charge	Total Charges
MATHEWS	39	14.25	56.37
BLOOM	54	10	68.32
HUTTON	138	0	149.04
LEWIS	77	28.5	111.66

Number of Customers   4
Total Rental Charges   266
Total Chemical Charges   42
Total Transportation Charges: 52.75
Total Customer Charges: 385.39

CHAPTER 4

Conditional Processing

Conditional Processing	48
IF Statement	48
Relational Operators	49
Sample Logical Expressions	49
Program Logic	54
Nested IF Statements	55
Compound Conditions	59
Priority	59
Summary	60
Review Questions	61

Conditional Processing

Up till now our programs have been relatively simple. We have used only two structures:

> Sequence
>
> Looping

The programs have handled each record in exactly the same manner. Most problems, however, require certain operations be performed only if certain conditions exist. For example:

- pay a salesman a bonus only if his sales for a period exceed the bonus limit;

- charge an athletic fee to full time students only;

- print people's names on a voters' list only if they are 18 years of age or older and they are Canadian citizens.

These are called **CONDITIONAL OPERATIONS** as they only take place when a certain condition exists (is true). It is the computer's ability to test for certain conditions, and select the appropriate action depending on the condition, that is referred to as **logical** decisions. This gives rise to the third structure allowed in structured programming:

> Selection

IF Statement

In Basic the selection type of conditional processing is done with an IF statement. In general form the statement is:

| IF | Logical Expression to be evaluated to TRUE or FALSE value | THEN | Action to be performed if the logical expression is TRUE |

The logical expression can be either **true** or **false**. Simple logical expressions consist of three parts:

A	B	C
Variable or Arithmetic Expression or Literal/ Constant	Relational Operator	Variable or Arithmetic Expression or Literal/ Constant

The expression to the left (A) is compared to the expression to the right (C) using the relational operator (B).

Relational Operators

=	Equal To
>	Greater Than
<	Less Than
>=	Greater Than or Equal To
<=	Less Than or Equal To
<>	Not Equal

Sample Logical Expressions

```
AGE = 19
SEX$ = "FEMALE"
AMOUNT * .08 <MINIMUM
SURNAME$ <>OLD.SURNAME$
```

Data types must be the same in both halves (A and C) of a logical expression. Numerics may only be compared with numerics, and strings may only be compared with strings. Numerics may be numeric variables, or constants (i.e., 19), or numeric expressions (i.e., AMOUNT * .08). Strings may be string variables ($ on end of variable name), or literals (i.e., string in quotes such as "FEMALE").

Strings are compared according to the ASCII Collating sequence, which is similar to the way one would find names arranged in a phone book.

Example:
> adams < black
> smith < smithson
> a > A

There are **four** main varieties of the IF statement. Each is shown with a sample flowchart and code.

1. Single Statement - Taking or not taking an action

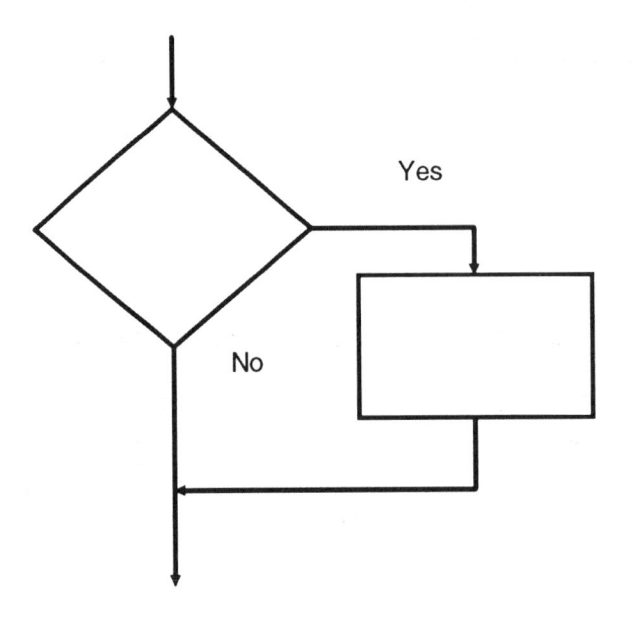

IF AGE >= 19 THEN PRINT SURNAME$;" IS OF AGE"

The statement(s) following the word THEN will only be executed if the condition is **true**. If the contents of the variable AGE are less than 19 then the statement(s) following the word THEN will *not* be executed.

2. Single Statement - Taking either of two actions

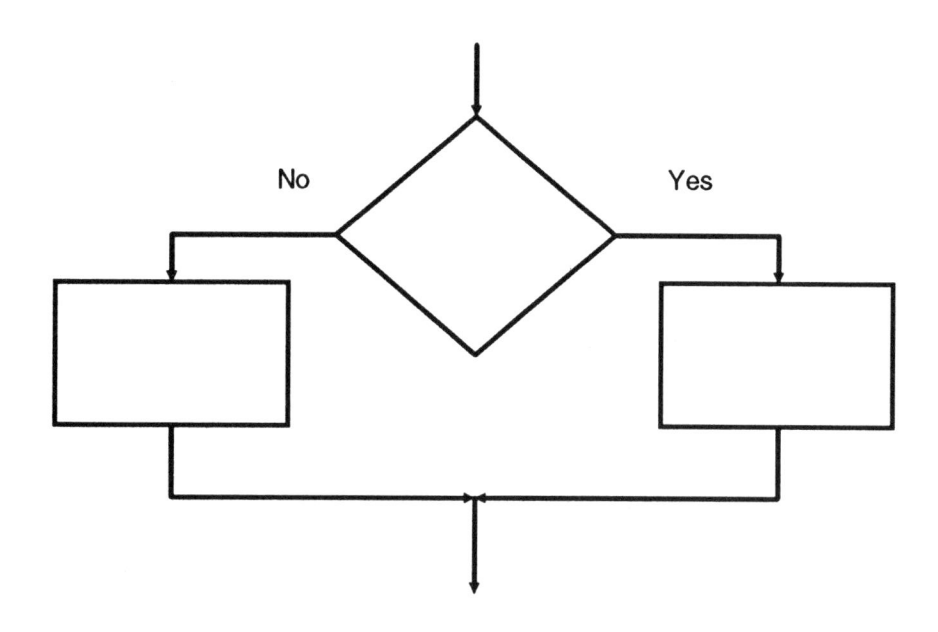

IF SALES > LIMIT **THEN** BONUS = 1000 **ELSE** BONUS = 0

If the condition is **true** the statements between the THEN and ELSE will be executed and statements following the ELSE are bypassed. If the condition is **false** the statements between the THEN and ELSE are bypassed, and only the statement(s) after the ELSE are executed.

3. Multi-Statement, Block mode - Taking or not taking a block of actions

This type of IF format is similar to format 1 above. The block mode version would be used in the case where there is **more than 1 action** to be done when the condition is true.

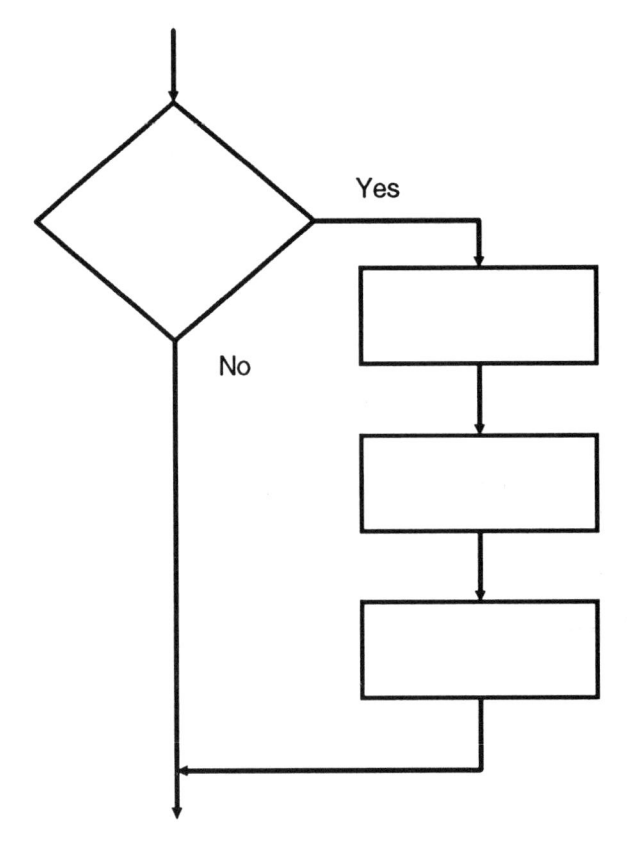

```
IF SALES > LIMIT THEN
        BONUS = 1000
        COUNT.BONUS = COUNT.BONUS + 1
        TOTAL.BONUS.PAID = TOTAL.BONUS.PAID + 1000
END IF
```

The statement(s) following the word THEN and before the END IF will only be executed if the condition is **true** (i.e. the contents of the variable SALES is greater than the contents of the variable LIMIT). Otherwise, if the condition is not true these statement(s) will be skipped, and execution will jump directly to the statement after the END IF.

4. Multi-Statement, Block mode - Taking one of two blocks of actions

This type of IF format is similar to format 2. The block mode version would be used in the case where there is **more than 1 action** to be done in either the true or false case.

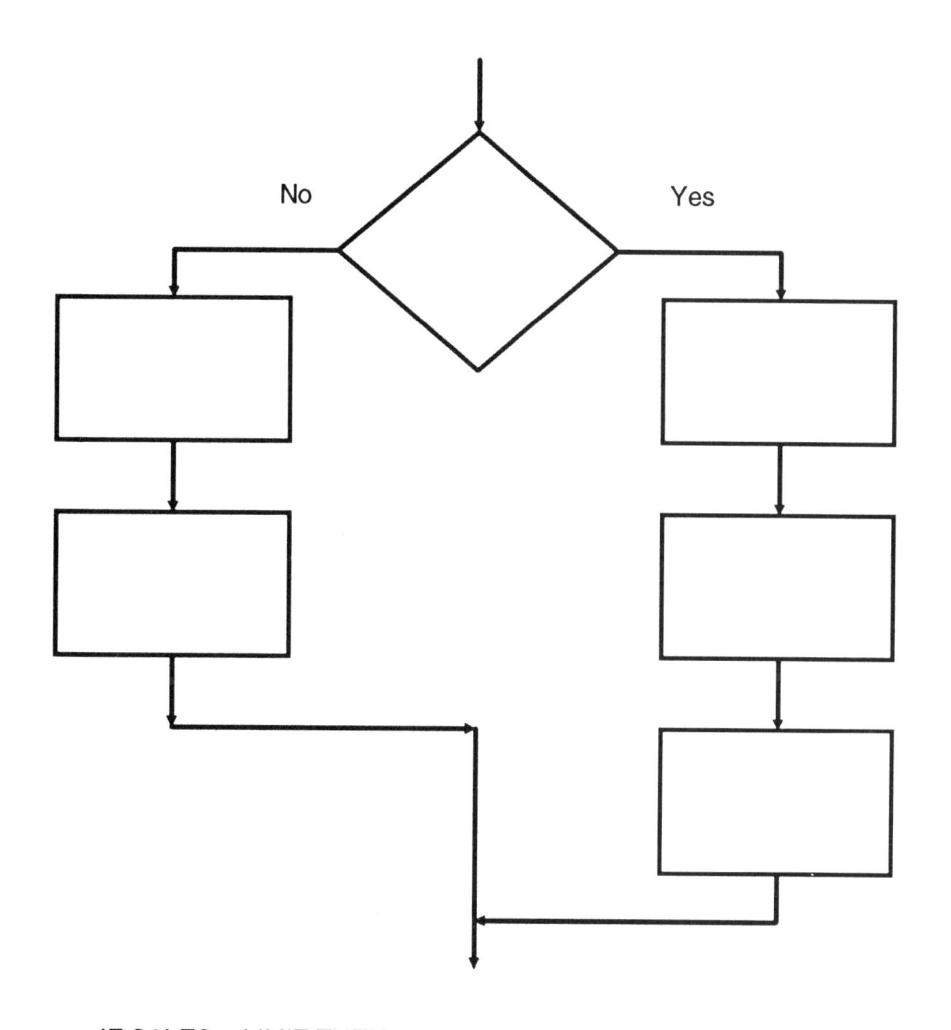

```
IF SALES > LIMIT THEN
        BONUS = 1000
        COUNT.BONUS = COUNT.BONUS + 1
        TOTAL.BONUS.PAID = TOTAL.BONUS.PAID + 1000
ELSE
        BONUS = 0
        COUNT.NO.BONUS = COUNT.NO.BONUS + 1
END IF
```

The statement(s) following the word THEN and before the ELSE will only be executed if the condition is **true** (i.e. the contents of the variable SALES is greater than the contents of the variable LIMIT), and the statements between the ELSE and END IF will be skipped. Otherwise, if the condition is not true the statements between the THEN and ELSE will be skipped and instead the statements between the ELSE and END IF will be executed. In either case execution will continue after the END IF.

Program Logic

IF statements must be used whenever the situation arises in a problem that requires certain actions only to be performed in certain cases. The IF statement works like a gate, directing execution to continue on certain paths depending on conditions. The statements that are executed depending on the condition should be indented at least three spaces so that they stand out. This makes it clear these statements are not part of the unconditional (always) processing of the program.

Conditional totaling and counting is a common application of the IF statement. In many problems a count or total of only a certain portion of the data is required. In examples 3 and 4 conditional counts of the number of people receiving bonus and the number of people not receiving bonus are calculated. This is achieved by using the same type of statement as was used for unconditional counts (counts of everything). The statement /COUNT.BONUS = COUNT.BONUS + 1/ causes the value of 1 to be added to the count. By putting this statement inside an IF statement the programmer has controlled the number of times the statement is executed. In format 4 on the previous page, the statement to increment COUNT.BONUS will only be executed in the case where SALES are greater than LIMIT. Similarly COUNT.NO.BONUS (another counter variable) will only be incremented when SALES are not greater than LIMIT. Thus at the end of the processing the variable COUNT.BONUS contains the number of bonuses paid, and COUNT.NO.BONUS contains the number of employees that did not get paid a bonus.

The same approach was used for accumulating total bonus paid. The statement to add to the variable TOTAL.BONUS.PAID is only included in the section of the IF statement to be executed when SALES are greater than LIMIT. There is no statement to increment the total in the portion of the IF to be executed if SALES is not greater than LIMIT, because no bonus is paid in this case.

Conditional processing is a difficult concept to grasp. Each problem that requires conditional processing must be evaluated as to which actions should be performed under which conditions. Program design using pseudocode or flowcharts is critical to the understanding of the problem. The best approach to ensure that your logic is correct is to trace the execution of your program using sample data.

Nested IF Statements

IF statements may be coded **within** other IF statements. The term given to this is NESTING. It is the act of putting one IF statement completely inside of another IF statement. It could be visualized as one nest that fits inside of another. It is used in the case where the statements to be executed depend on more that one condition. It is best illustrated by an example that requires nested IFs.

Problem:

Records in the data file contain a student's name, a code character (F for full-time student, or P for part-time), a country shortform (CAN for Canadian, or the shortform for another country), and the number of courses taken. The program is to calculate student fees. The fees schedule is as follows:

FULL TIME STUDENTS - Canadian $100/course

                                  - Foreign $150/course

PART TIME STUDENTS - Canadian $50/course

                                  - Foreign $85/course

Data to be output for each record (student) is student name, FULL TIME or PART TIME (depending on code), and their fees. At the end of the report print a summary including the number of full-time students, the number of part-time students, the total fees for Canadian students, and the total fees for foreign students.

Discussion

What actions should be done conditionally in this program? The count of full-time and part-time students must be incremented depending on the type code. The words FULL TIME and PART TIME are required in the output and must be set depending on the type code of the record being processed. The fees are calculated depending on type code and citizenship. The total Canadian student fees and foreign student fees must be incremented depending on the citizenship of the record being processed.

All of this conditional processing is done in the PROCESS routine. The flowchart and code for the PROCESS routine are shown on the next pages. Note the use of comments embedded in the code. This helps the programmer, and others who read the code later, to better understand the logic.

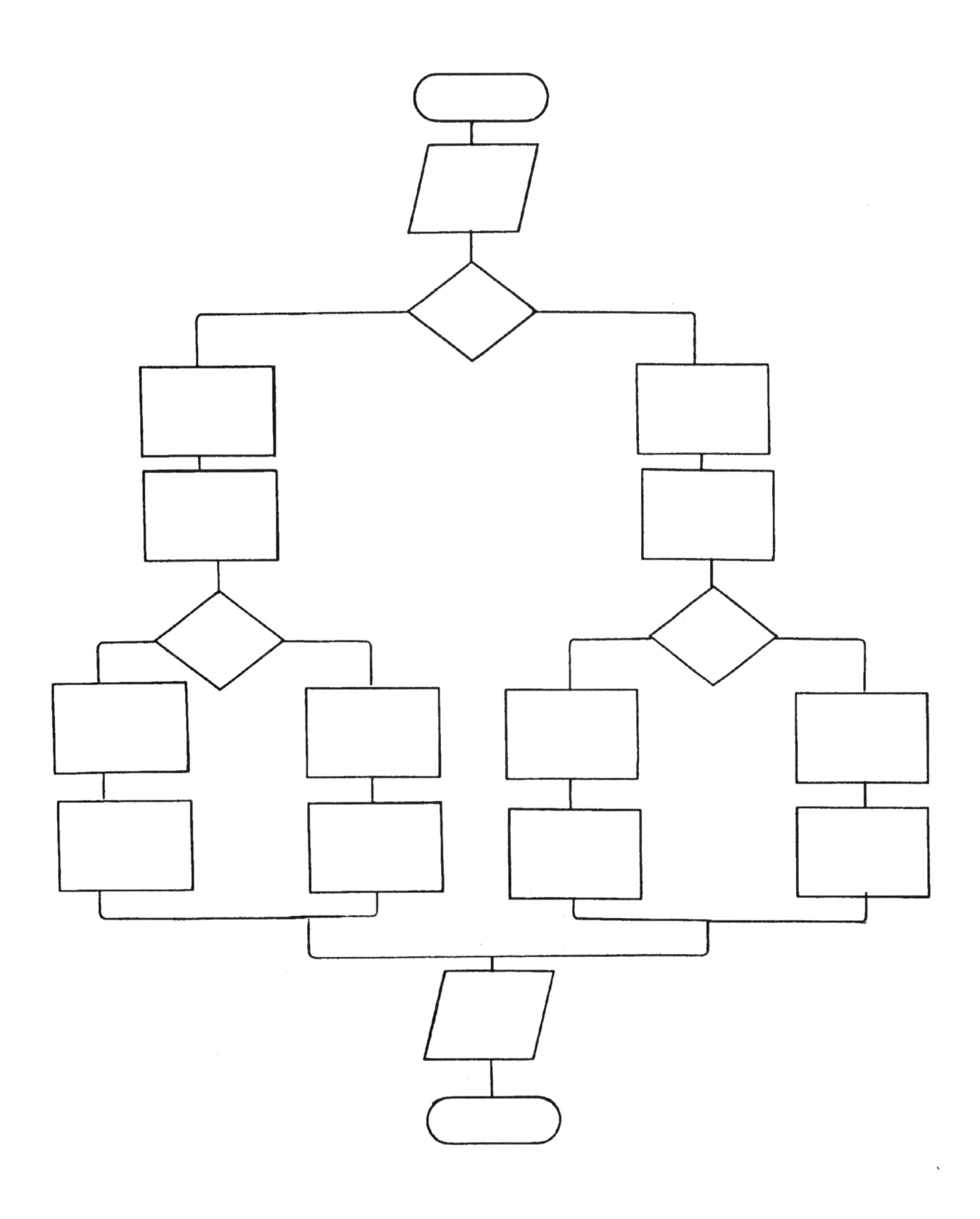

CODE

```
' Process routine
'~~~~~~~
  PROCESS:
  INPUT #1,STUDENT.NAME$,CODE$,COUNTRY$,NUM.COURSES
  IF CODE$ = "F" THEN                         ' *** FULL TIME
    CODEWORD$ = "FULL TIME"
    FULL.COUNT = FULL.COUNT + 1
    IF COUNTRY$ = "CAN" THEN                  ' ... CAN
       FEES = NUM.COURSES * 100
       TOTAL.CAN.FEES = TOTAL.CAN.FEES + FEES
    ELSE                                      ' ... OTHER
       FEES = NUM.COURSES * 150
       TOTAL.FOREIGN.FEES = TOTAL.FOREIGN.FEES +FEES
    END IF
  ELSE                                        ' *** PART TIME
    CODEWORD$ = "PART TIME"
    PARTTIME.COUNT = PARTTIME.COUNT + 1
    IF COUNTRY$ = "CAN" THEN                  ' ... CAN
       FEES = NUM.COURSES * 50
       TOTAL.CAN.FEES = TOTAL.CAN.FEES + FEES
    ELSE                                      ' ... OTHER
       FEES = NUM.COURSES * 85
       TOTAL.FOREIGN.FEES = TOTAL.FOREIGN.FEES + FEES
    END IF
  END IF
  LPRINT STUDENT.NAME$,CODEWORD$,FEES
  RETURN
```

Compound Conditions

The two most common **logical operators** that may be used to build compound or combined conditions are AND and OR. They are interpreted much the same as they are in English. The reason that they prove to be difficult to code, even though we use them daily in English, is that we are not very precise in our English use of them.

AND:

When two conditions are combined with an **AND** then both of the individual conditions must be true for the combined condition to be considered true.

Sample:

    IF AGE >18 AND CITIZENSHIP$ = "CAN" THEN LPRINT NAM$

The combined condition above could be used to screen people for a voters' list. Only those people who were Canadian citizens and whose age was > 18 would be printed on the voters list.

OR:

When two conditions are combined with an **OR** then if either one of the conditions is true the combined condition will be considered true.

Sample:

    IF SEX$ = "FEMALE" OR AGE < 13 THEN LPRINT NAM$

The combined condition above could be used to select all women and children from the data. Note that the use of OR will allow male children to be part of the selection as well as female children.

Priority

When both AND and OR exist in the same condition, the AND takes priority and is evaluated before the OR. This is similar to the order of operations in an arithmetic expression where multiplication and division are evaluated before addition and subtraction. As with arithmetic, bracketed conditions **always take highest priority** and are evaluated first. Because compound conditions are confusing at the best of time, it is **always** wise to include brackets to clearly indicate the order of evaluating conditions.

Sample:

> IF SEX$ = "M" AND AGE <19 OR AGE >65   THEN LPRINT NAM$
>> selects all young males and seniors of either sex

> IF SEX$ = "M" AND (AGE <19 OR AGE >65) THEN LPRINT NAM$
>> selects only young and old males (i.e. no females of any age and no men aged from 19 to 65)

Summary

Conditional processing can get complicated. The best way to approach problem solving with conditional processing is to follow the guidelines below:

- Recognize when you need conditional operations.

- Decide on the condition(s).

- Decide what you need to do when the condition is true and/or false.

- Design the program (flowchart or pseudocode). Include all actions that are to be performed conditionally as part of the IF structure. Do not include anything in the IF structure if it doesn't need to be there. If it is an action that should always be performed, leave it out of the IF structure.

- Code the program.

- Use indentation between the IF ELSE and END IF statements.

- Use remarks to clarify logic.

- Don't forget the END IF to signal the end of the IF structure.

Review Questions

1. List all the relational operators.

2. List two logical operators.

3. State which of the following are invalid if statements and why.

    a)   AGE > 19 OR < 65 THEN PRINT NAM$

    b)   IF SEX$ = MALE THEN PRINT "MAN"

    c)   IF FIRST$ = "no" AND AGE > 65 THEN

       COUNT = COUNT + 1

      ELSE THEN

       SENIOR.CNT = SENIOR.CNT + 1

      END IF

4. Explain what data the records must contain so that the variable COUNT will be incremented based on the following IF statements.

    a)   IF GRADE$ = "A" AND AGE <= 20 THEN

       COUNT = COUNT + 1

      END IF

    b)   IF GRADE$ <> "A" OR SEX$ = "M" THEN

       COUNT = COUNT + 1

      END IF

    c)   IF AGE > 20 AND SEX$="M" OR SEX$ = "F" THEN

       COUNT = COUNT + 1

      END IF

    d)   IF AGE >=20 AND (SEX$ = "M" OR SEX$ = "F") THEN

       COUNT = COUNT + 1

      END IF

5. Given that the variable AGE contains a person's age, and the variable MARRIED$ contains a marital status as follows:

   "M" - married
   "D" - divorced
   "W" - widowed
   "S" - single.

   Write the IF statement to increment the count only for senior citizens (age >=65) who were at one time or are still married.

6. Write the Basic code for the PROCESS routine only for the following program.

   A record of a college class file includes the following:

   course name
   course number
   maximum allowed enrolment
   actual enrolment

   A report is to be printed that includes only those courses that are over-enrolled. For each such course print:

   Course number, course name, the message OVER ENROLLED BY, and the number of excess students.

   At the end of the report print the number of courses that are over-enrolled.

   Enhancement: - modify the code to also accumulate the number of courses that are not over enrolled to be printed at the end of the report.

Programming Problems:

Problem #1 - General Ledger Transaction Report

INSTRUCTIONS:

A program is required to process the General Ledger transaction file for a company and print out a transaction record report.

INPUT:

The input data will be provided in a filed called GLTRX.DAT, and will consist of records containing three fields; account number, account description, and transaction amount. If the transaction amount is a Debit the amount will be a **positive** value. If it is a Credit it will be a **negative** value. A sample of the records is shown below:

Account Number	Account Name	Transaction Amount
1-0010	Cash	1238.90
1-2050	Accounts Rec.	56789.03
2-5409	Depreciation	-3456.78

OUTPUT:

Output is a report listing all of the GL Transactions with the debit amounts printed in one column, and the credit amounts printed in another. The program should also determine the total of the debits, and the total of the credits and the total number of GL transactions in the file. These results will be printed at the end of the report.

The output report might look like the example printed on the next page:

Smith, Smith & Smith Attorneys
General Ledger Transaction Report

Account Number	Account Description	Debit	Credit
1-0010	Cash	1238.9	
1-2050	Accounts Rec.	56789.03	
2-5409	Depreciation		3456.78

Total Debits................ 58027.93
Total Credits............... 3456.78
Number of Transactions...... 3

Problem #2 - Campsite Charges

INSTRUCTIONS:

A report is to be prepared of campsite charges for vehicles. A program should be designed and coded in BASIC to produce the report.

INPUT:

Input consists of records containing the vehicle licence plate number, the length of the camper in feet, the number of days that they will be staying, and a flag with a status of either Y or N indicating whether they are members of the campground or not (i.e. Y - Yes a member, and N - Non-member). Build a sequential data file containing the following data.

LICENCE NUMBER	LENGTH OF CAMPER (FEET)	NUMBER OF DAYS STAY	MEMBER FLAG
RST 909	12	6	N
LOV 881	18	3	Y
CIM 098	24	2	Y
VEL 636	9	5	N
TTU 651	36	5	N
UST 897	14	7	Y

OUTPUT:

Output is a report of the money collected from campsite registration for the day. If the camper is a member of the campground and has a large camper (more than 15 feet) then the charge is $12.84 per day. If the camper is a non member and has a large camper (more than 15 feet) then the charge is $16.05 per day. If the camper is a member with a small camper (15 feet or less) then the charge is $8.03 per day. If the camper is a non- member and the camper is small (15 feet or less) then the charge is $10.63 per day. The format of the output is illustrated below. After all records in the file have been processed, summary totals are to be given as illustrated below.

Sample output for Problem #2

```
           Peaceful Lake Campground
             Campsite Registration
Campsite   License   Member    Number of    Charge
Size                            Days
Small Site   RST 909     N         6         $ 63.78
Large Site   LOV 881     Y         3         $ 38.52
Large Site   CIM 098     Y         2         $ 25.68
Small Site   VEL 636     N         5         $ 53.15
Large Site   TTU 651     N         5         $ 80.25
Small Site   UST 897     Y         7         $ 56.21
Number of Vehicles       6
Small Site Income      173.14
Large Site Income      144.45
Total Income           317.59
```

Problem #3 - Toll Bridge Charges

INSTRUCTIONS:

A report is to be prepared of toll bridge charges for vehicles. A program should be designed and coded in BASIC to produce the report.

INPUT:

Input consists of records containing the type of vehicle, the licence plate number, the province, and the number of passengers in the vehicle. An automobile is identified by the code A, and a truck by the code T. All records will contain either a code A or a code T. Build a sequential data file containing the following data.

VEHICLE	LICENSE	PROVINCE	NUMBER OF PASSENGERS
A	RST 909	ONT	3
T	LOV 881	NFLD	1
T	CIM 098	ONT	3
A	VEL 636	SASK	5
T	TTU 651	QUE	1
A	UST 897	ONT	3

OUTPUT:

Output is a report of the money collected from the toll bridge for the day. If the vehicle is an automobile from the province of Ontario (ONT), the charge is 65 cents per person. If the vehicle is an automobile from a province other than Ontario, the charge is 75 cents per person. If the vehicle is a truck from the province of Ontario, the charge is $1.25 per person. If the vehicle is a truck from a province other than Ontario the charge is $1.75 per person. The format of the output is illustrated on the next page. After all records in the file have been processed, a summary report is to be prepared as illustrated on the next page.

```
                    DAILY
                TOLL BRIDGE REPORT
        VEHICLE    LICENCE    PROVINCE    CHARGE
        AUTO       RST 909    ONT         $ 1.95
        TRUCK      LOV 881    NFLD        $ 1.75
        TRUCK      CIM 098    ONT         $ 3.75
        AUTO       VEL 636    SASK        $ 3.75
        TRUCK      TTU 651    QUE         $ 1.75
        AUTO       UST 897    ONT         $ 1.95
                   SUMMARY
        TOTAL      TOTAL      TRUCK       AUTO
        VEHICLES   PEOPLE     INCOME      INCOME
        6          16         $ 7.25      $ 7.65
```

CHAPTER 5

Report Improvement

Improving The Appearance of Printed Reports	**69**
Horizontal Print Spacing	**69**
TAB Function	**70**
SPC Function	**70**
DATE$ Function	**71**
Print Using Statement	**71**
Combining Edit Masks	**75**
Separate Coding of Edit Masks	**76**
Report Layout	**77**
Program Design	**77**
Enhanced Program with Edit Masks	**78**
Review Questions	**79**

Improving the Appearance of Printed Reports

The printed reports that have been generated to this point are complete in the data that they contain, but the format and layout leave much to be desired. Report layout has been restricted to 5 zones, each 14 positions wide. In many instances these 5 zones are not sufficient, or leave too much wasted space. Columns of numeric data are accurate, but appear messy because decimal places are not lined up vertically. Headings are crude and do not contain important information such as current time and date.

Standard printer paper size is 8 1/2 inches wide by 11 inches long. Standard print lines are 6 per inch, allowing 66 printed lines per page. The normal character pitch will allow 80 characters to print in one line on the screen and printer. Choosing different character pitches and lines per inch would allow different report layouts, but for the purpose of reports in this book a standard page of 80 character positions in width and 66 lines long will be assumed.

Horizontal Print Spacing

Up till now the only tool we have used to position data for printing is by separating the items in a print statement with either a comma or a semicolon. Commas cause output to be printed in 14 character zones, and semicolons cause output to be printed close together.

Any print statement that ends with a comma or semicolon will effectively "hold" that output line, and the output from the PRINT statement executed next will be added to the end of the previous output.

Sample:
```
PRINT "HI";
PRINT " THERE"
```

causes output:

```
HI THERE
```

(all on the same line - the trailing ';' prevents the carriage return and line feed)

TAB Function:

Two functions are available for specific character placement on a line. The TAB(n) function allows you to specify the exact character position that the next item will be printed at in a PRINT or LPRINT statement. The position is specified as a number or numeric variable in brackets after TAB. Most programmers find TAB especially useful in positioning titles and headings.

Sample:

```
LPRINT TAB(5);"WIDGETS LTD.";TAB(20);"MONTHLY PAYROLL"
causes output:
position 1...5....10........20................
            WIDGETS LTD.   MONTHLY PAYROLL
```

If the numeric value used in the TAB function is less that the current print position, then Basic will drop to the next line in order to print the data at the specified position. For example, if the second TAB function in the above statement was TAB(10) instead of TAB(20) then MONTHLY PAYROLL would be printed starting at position 20 on the next line after the line containing WIDGETS LTD. Similarly, semicolons should be used instead of commas in a PRINT statement containing TABs. If commas are used then Basic will skip to the next 14 position zone before attempting to advance to the TAB. In many cases this could leave the print position beyond the TAB position, causing output to drop to the next line.

SPC Function:

The SPC(n) function is similar to the TAB(n) function, except that it causes printing to **space over** a specified number of positions, rather than to a specific position.

Sample:

```
PRINT SPC(5);"WIDGETS LTD.";SPC(8);"MONTHLY PAYROLL"
causes output:
position 1...5....10........20................
            WIDGETS LTD.        MONTHLY PAYROLL
```

DATE$ Function

If a date is hard coded as part of a program (i.e. PRINT "Jan. 12/91"), then whenever that program is run the same date will print. This is not particularly useful from a reporting standpoint as usually it is desirable to print the current system date as supplied by the computer as part of a report. The DATE$ function may be thought of as a specially designated variable that always automatically contains the current system date in the form MM-DD-YYYY. Note that the $ designates this as a **string** function (i.e., a function that returns a character value as opposed to a pure numeric value). The DATE$ function may be used in a PRINT statement to print the date, just as any other literal or variable is used.

Sample:

```
PRINT TAB(5);DATE$;TAB(20);"WIDGETS LTD."

causes output:

position 1...5....10........20................
            06-18-1991      WIDGETS LTD.
```

Print Using Statement:

Lining up decimal points in a column of numeric values is not possible with simple print statements. Long string fields such as names may also throw out column printing using zones, as longer strings will cause printing of subsequent fields in farther print zones rather than shorter fields. If you want to take complete control over the way your output is printed, then you must use the PRINT USING statement. The PRINT USING statement uses a set of codes stored in an **edit mask** to control where each character of the output will be positioned. The edit mask may be visualized as a stencil or mask dictating the positioning.

Format:

    PRINT USING   mask;   list of items to print

Sample:

```
PRINT USING "######.##"; STOCK.VALUE
```
causes output:

```
        contents of variable         output
           STOCK.VALUE              1...5....10........20
              43                          43.00
             512.3                       512.30
             3.211                         3.21
            72.468                        72.47
              .2                           0.20
           1000000                    %1000000
```

Each # in the edit mask represents one digit of output. When the value is printed in the given edit mask it will be aligned around the decimal point (or implied decimal point in the case of an edit mask without a decimal ... ### has an implied decimal at the end).

Rules governing display of values in a numeric edit mask:

- A digit will be printed in all positions following the decimal point (i.e. trailing zeros after the decimal will be displayed).

- Leading zeroes are displayed as spaces.

- Decimal positions will be rounded to fit in the edit mask.

- If a value is too large to fit in the edit mask a % will be printed in front of it.

Other special symbols may be inserted in numeric edit masks:

One , (**comma**) anywhere to the left of a decimal point in a numeric edit mask will cause commas to be inserted in the thousands, millions etc. as required by the value.

Sample:

```
PRINT USING "######,.##"; STOCK.VALUE
```
causes output:

```
        contents of variable        output
        STOCK.VALUE                 1...5....10........20
        276.3                              276.30
        1143                             1,143.00
        1000000                          %1000000
```

Two $ (dollar signs) coded at the start of a numeric edit mask will place a floating $ in front of the first digit of the output.

```
PRINT USING "$$####,.##"; STOCK.VALUE
```
causes output:

```
        contents of variable        output
        STOCK.VALUE                 1...5....10........20
        43.3                              $43.30
        1000                           $1,000.00
```

Sample:

Two * (asterisks) at the start of a numeric edit mask causes the unused numeric positions to be filled with *s. This is useful for cheques to prevent someone from altering the amount.

Sample:

```
PRINT USING "**####.##"; CHEQUE.VALUE
```
causes output:

```
        contents of variable        output
        CHEQUE.VALUE                1...5....10........20
        43.3                        ****43.30
```

One - (minus sign) coded at the end of a numeric edit mask will cause negative values to be printed with a trailing minus sign, and positive values to be printed with a trailing space.

Sample:

```
PRINT USING "####,.##-"; BALANCE
causes output:
        contents of variable      output
        BALANCE                   1...5....10........20
        43.3                         43.30-
        3251.2                    3,251.20
```

Strings:

The preceding edit characters were for printing numeric values. String values must be printed in different edit masks.

The edit mask for a string of two or more characters is composed of backslashes separated by the desired number of spaces. The total number of positions for the string is the total length of the edit mask (including both the backslashes and spaces). If the string is shorter than the length of the edit mask the string is left justified and padded with spaces. If the string is too long to fit in the edit mask the extra characters to the right are truncated (not displayed).

Sample: (. is used to represent a space)

```
PRINT USING "\......\"; ITEM.NAME$
causes output:
        contents of variable      output
        ITEM.NAME$                1...5....10........20
        Bat                       Bat.....
        Volley Ball               Volley B
```

String edit mask for a string of only one character could therefore not be represented using backslashes. Instead a ! (exclamation mark) is used for a string mask of 1 character.

Sample:

```
PRINT USING "!"; SEX$
```
causes output:

```
        contents of variable        output
        SEX$                        1...5....10........20
        Male                        M
        Female                      F
```

Combining Edit Masks

The edit masks developed above are useful only for single fields. When creating a report several edit masks are combined to create the format for an entire line of output. Blank spaces are left between the individual masks to indicate the number of positions to be left blank between output fields. Text may also be included in the edit mask. The text will print in the exact positions as shown in the mask. Be careful to avoid any special editing characters in the text as they will be interpreted as editing features and not text unless preceded by an underline character.

Sample:

```
PRINT USING "\...........\  ##,### ####.## #######,.##";
          ITEM.NAME$, QTY.ON.HAND, ITEM.COST, STOCK.VALUE
```
causes output:

```
Hockey Stick        23    18.75        431.25
```

Sample:

```
PRINT USING "TOTAL STOCK VALUE: $$#########,.##";TOTAL.STOCK.VALUE
```
causes output like

```
TOTAL STOCK VALUE:       $81,362.83
```

When using an edit mask with multiple edits, the type of the edit mask must agree with the data to be printed in the mask. For example, in the first mask above the edit masks were respectively; String, Numeric, Numeric, Numeric, and likewise the data to be printed in the masks were of the same type in the same order; String, Numeric, Numeric and Numeric.

Although the first sample above showed a print statement that appeared to span two lines, the user would have had to code it as one line, wrapped around, without pressing the return key at the end of the first physical line. QBASIC will allow statements up to 256 characters long. A statement is ended by pressing the return key. A single statement may therefore span 80 character screen lines, as long as the user does not press the return key until the end of the completed statement.

Separate Coding of Edit Masks

The above concept of an Edit Mask for more than one data field may be taken yet another step further. The Edit Mask portion of the PRINT USING statement may be stored in a separate string variable, and used later in execution in a PRINT USING statement, by simply providing the name of the string variable containing the Edit Mask where the Edit Mask would be coded. Typical names for string variables containing Edit Masks are D1$, D2$, D3$, etc. The letter D is used to indicate Detail line. String variables are also commonly used for headings, and titles. They are commonly named H1$, H2$, etc.

Sample:

```
D1$="\.............\    ##,###    ####.##    #########,.##"
PRINT USING D1$; ITEM.NAME$, QTY.ON.HAND, ITEM.COST, STOCK.VALUE
```

Where would the user include this code to assign Edit Masks and headings to variables? Think about the order of execution. The Edit Masks and headings would have to be assigned to string variables before they are referenced in a PRINT STATEMENT. Also, they would only need to be assigned to the variables once in the program. Using the variables does not destroy their contents, but leaves it intact for repeated use.

The logical place to assign Edit Masks and Headings to string variables would therefore have to be in the INIT routine, as it contains the actions that are done one time only, before the processing of the data is done.

The Edit Masks and Heading string variables would be used later in the program, when headings are printed and detail lines and total lines are printed.

Report Layout

The user must spend time organizing and laying out the format of the output before coding. This task can be simplified by using a report layout form and manually printing the headings and masks on that form, so that the output will line up appropriately.

Another way that is even faster is to lay out the design of the report directly on the screen while entering the QBASIC program. First enter the headings and Edit Masks, using the full 80-character width of the screen. Do not generate real Basic Statements with quotes around the strings, or the "variable = " portion of the statements. When the layout appears just the way you want it on the screen, go back, and with INSERT ON, add the "variable = ", quotes and statement indentation to turn the layout lines into assignment statements.

Program Design

Both flowcharts and pseudocode are purposefully vague in their description of layout of program output. For this reason, only one minor modification need be made to flowcharts or pseudocode to incorporate edit masks.

In the design for the **INIT** routine, include an assignment box (for flowcharts) or action (for pseudocode) entitled:

> Setup headings and Edit Masks

Enhanced Basic Program with Edit Masks

```
' Program    : CH5EX1.BAS
' Programmer : Kristin Higgins
' Date       : June 14, 1990
' Data File  : CH5EX1.DAT
' Purpose    : To read records from the sports inventory file
'            : and print a report listing the value of the
'            : stock. Program uses edit masks for printing
'            : headings, detail lines, and total lines.
'
' Mainline
' --------
  gosub init
  do until eof(1)
    gosub process
  loop
  gosub terminate
  end

' Init Routine
' ------------
init:

  open "A:CH5EX1.DAT" for input as #1

  h1$ = "\              \     SPORTS EXMPORIUM STOCK REPORT"
  h2$ = "ITEM                 QUANTITY          ITEM              STOCK"
  h3$ = "NAME                 ON  HAND          COST              VALUE"
  d1$ = "\              \    ##,###          #####,.##      #######,.##"
  t1$ = "Number of Items   :     ###,###"
  t2$ = "Total Stock Value : $$#######,.##"
  lprint using h1$;date$
  lprint
  lprint h2$
  lprint h3$
  lprint
  item.count = 0
  total.stock.value = 0
  return

' Process Routine
' ---------------
process:

  input #1, item.name$, qty.on.hand, item.cost
  stock.value = qty.on.hand * item.cost
  lprint  using d1$; item.name$, qty.on.hand, item.cost, stock.value
  item.count = item.count + 1
  total.stock.value = total.stock.value + stock.value
  return

' Terminate Routine
' -----------------

terminate:

  lprint
  lprint using t1$; item.count
  lprint using t2$; total.stock.value
  lprint
  lprint "***** End of Report *****"
  return

' End of Program File
' -------------------
```

Output from CH5EX1.BAS

```
06-18-1991      SPORTS EXMPORIUM STOCK REPORT

ITEM            QUANTITY        ITEM        STOCK
NAME            ON  HAND        COST        VALUE

Hockey Stick         23        18.75       431.25
Badminton Net        11         5.75        63.25

Number of Items  :        2
Total Stock Value :   $494.50

***** End of Report *****
```

Review Questions

1. Indicate the exact output generated by the following statements. Use the symbol † to indicate a blank space.

    a) PRINT TAB(5);"January";SPC(4);"1992"

    b) PRINT "January",TAB(10);"1992"

2. Indicate how the following values would print in the given edit masks. Use † to represent a blank.

    a) EDIT MASK ###.##

    12

    453.322

    .1

    1.9999999999999

    44444

    0

    b) EDIT MASK $$#####,.##

    1.1

    10000

    50

    123456.789

    1234567.8

c)   EDIT MASK ###-

   1.234

   -30

   29

d)   EDIT MASK \†††††\   († represents a blank)

   Johnathon Wilson

   Bev

e)   EDIT MASK !

   Super

3. Given the following variable contents and edit mask, indicate the exact form of the output (using † for blank spaces).

   a) print using d1$; nam$, count, sex$, salary

   d1$ = "\††††\††###†††!†††$$####,.##"
   nam$ = "Sue"
   count = 41.9
   sex$ = "Female"
   salary = 13423

   b) print using h1$; date$, page.count

   h1$ = "\††††††††\††††††Kristin Limited††††Page ##"
   date$ = 01/01/1992
   page.count = 3

Programming Problems

Use Edit Masks to improve the appearance of printed reports generated from programming problems in the previous chapters. Position titles using TAB and SPC functions. Use edit masks for headings, detail lines, and final totals. Add dollar signs to all final totals, show commas in Thousands where appropriate, limit dollar amounts to two decimal places, and limit string output to the length allowed by the positioning of column headings.

CHAPTER 6

Page Breaks

Page Breaks	82
Page Layout	82
Program Logic	83
Line and Page Counters	83
Detecting Page Full	83
Page Eject and Headings	84
Coding	84
Enhanced Pseudocode for Page Breaks	86
Enhanced Basic Program for Page Breaks	87
Review Questions	89

Page Breaks

Up to this point, the data files we have dealt with have been relatively small, allowing the full report output to be less that one page in size. Typically, data files are larger than those we have worked with. Larger data files generate larger output. With continuous forms paper, reports that have output longer than one single page will print directly over the page perforations, without leaving blank lines at the top and bottom of each page.

Our programs should be enhanced to recognize the point where the current page of output is nearly filled with printing. At that point, the current printer page should be ejected, and printing continued on the next page. Margins of blank space should be left at the top and bottom of each page, and headings should be repeated at the top of the new page. Page numbers should be displayed in the headings.

Page Layout

The contents of a standard report may be divided into three main areas, as seen below; heading lines, detail lines, and summary (total) lines.

```
+------------------------------------------+
|                                          |
|       Section used for Page Headings     |
|_____|
|                                          |
|                                          |
|    Section used for the main body or de- |
|         tail portion of the report       |
|                                          |
|                                          |
|                                          |
|                                          |
|                                          |
|                                          |
|_____|
|                                          |
|   Section used for Page Summaries, if required |
+------------------------------------------+
```

Standard page length is 11 inches. Standard print size is 6 lines per inch. Thus there is room for 66 lines of printing on a page. Top and bottom margins of blank space are included to improve the appearance of the page. Typically, programmers will end the printing on the page somewhere in the area of the 55th line to allow for a bottom margin of blank space.

Program Logic

The first step is to add the logic to the program, to detect the point at which a page is full and eject to the next page. Following the scenario described above, consider that the page is full after 55 lines. In order to have a program know when 55 detail lines have been printed, we need a line counter.

Line and Page Counters

The concept of a counter is familiar to you. A line counter is no different from any other counter. The line counter will be incremented (increased by 1) every time a line is printed. Detail lines are printed in the PROCESS routine, therefore the line counter should be incremented in the PROCESS routine, whenever a line is printed.

The page counter would be initialized to 0 at the start of execution. It would be increased by 1 at the start of every page.

Detecting Page Full

Logic must be added to test the line counter before a detail line is printed. If the line counter is at the page full point (>= 55), then the page should be ejected and headings printed, before the next detail line is printed.

Where would the line counter be tested to see if the page is full? Since it must be done before the printing of the detail line, it must be added to the routine that prints the detail line (i.e. the PROCESS routine.) What type of statement would be used to check if the line counter has reached page full (55 lines)? Since we want to compare the contents of the line counter variable to 55, and perform the action of page eject and printing headings only when line counter exceeds 55, we use an IF statement:

```
IF LINE.COUNT >= 55 THEN  ........
```

Page Eject and Headings

What is it that you want the program to do to begin a new page?

- If not the first page eject to top of a new page.

- Add 1 to the page counter.

- Print the top page margin and headings.

- Set the line counter back to the number of lines printed for the top margin and heading, so as to begin counting for the new page.

The above actions may be grouped together as a sub-task that must be done at the start of each page. Top down design techniques suggest that these actions should constitute a subroutine.

The subroutine should be **invoked** from two places: in the INIT routine to start the first page, (to print headings on the first page), and then repeated whenever the number of detail lines printed has reached the maximum allowed per page.

Coding

All of the logic for page breaks can be coded using Basic statements already introduced in previous chapters, with one exception. There is a quick way to cause a page eject. A page of paper in the printer may be manually ejected by pressing the form feed button on the printer. The form feed control character is the ASCII character 12. To encode this in a program, simply output the ASCII character 12 as follows:

```
LPRINT CHR$(12)
```

The CHR$(n) is a function that generates the ASCII character with the value n.

Chapter 6 Page Breaks

Enhanced Flowchart for Page Breaks

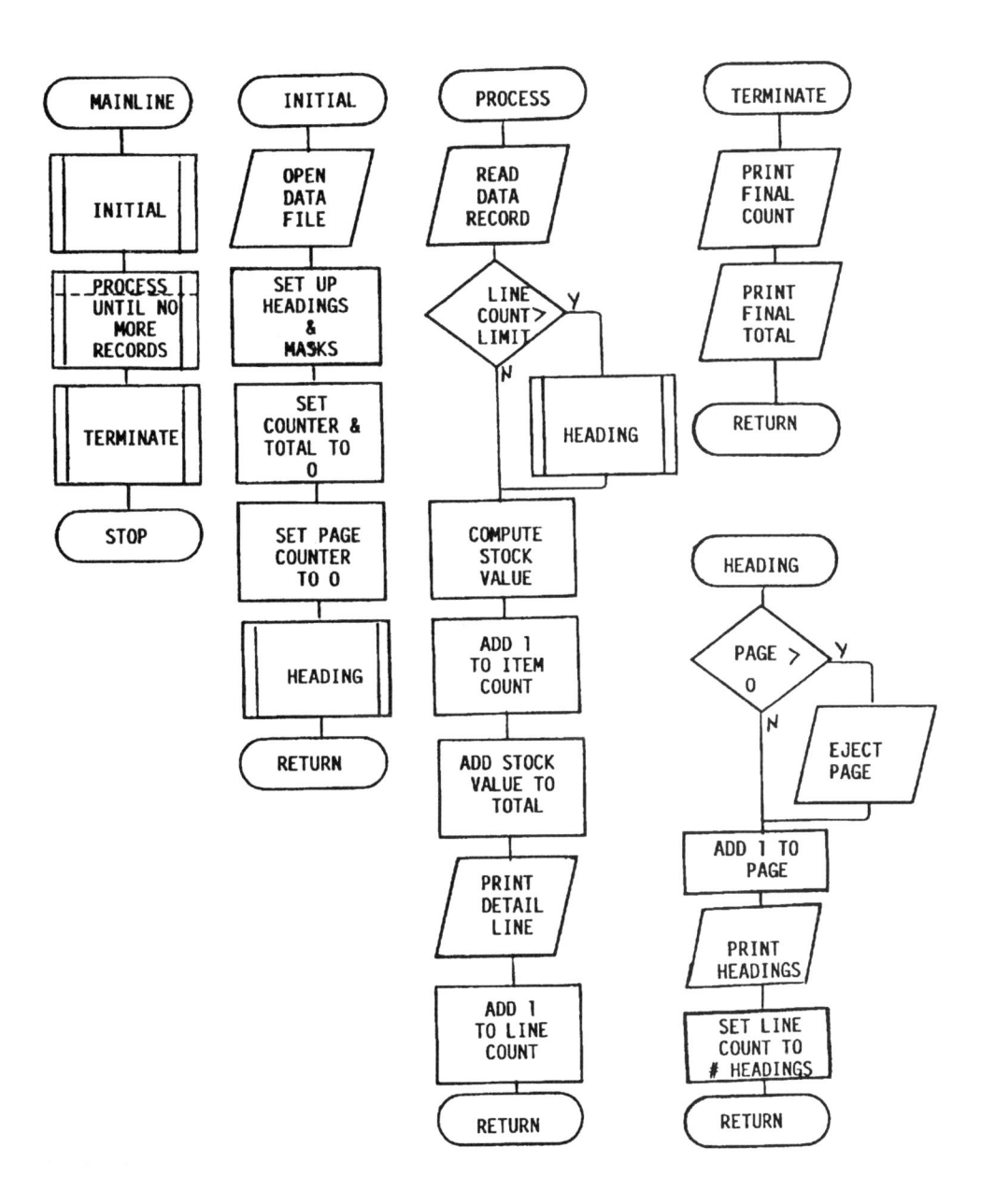

Enhanced Pseudocode for Page Breaks
VTOC

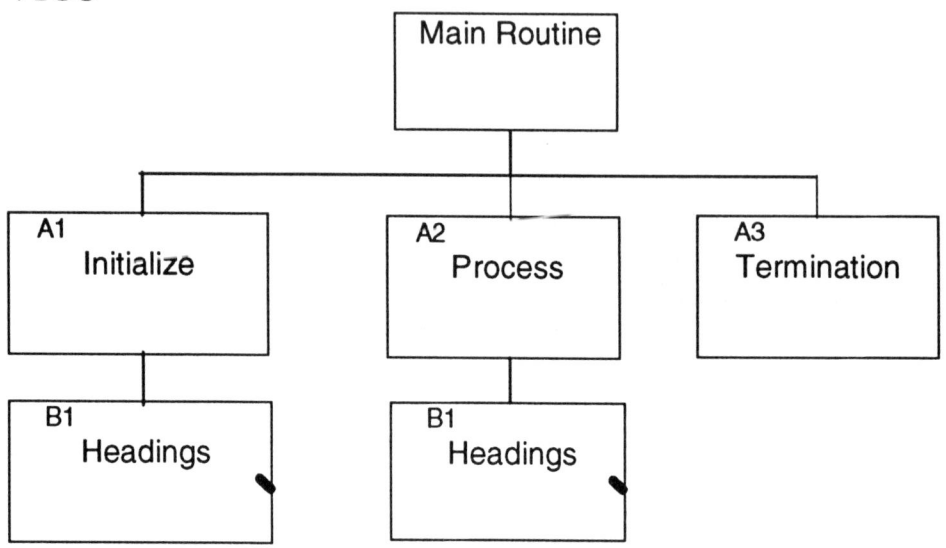

```
                    Main Routine
          ┌──────────────┼──────────────┐
      A1              A2              A3
   Initialize        Process       Termination
       │               │
      B1              B1
   Headings        Headings
```

Pseudocode

Mainline:
    Perform Initialization Routine
    Perform the Process Routine repeatedly until there are no more data records
    Perform the Termination Routine

Initialization:
    Open the data file
    Setup headings and edit masks
    Initialize item counter and total to 0

Process:
    Read data record
    Initialize Page counter
    Perform Heading routine
    Compute stock value = unit cost x quantity on hand
    Increase item count by 1
    If line counter exceeds page length perform Heading routine
    Increase total stock value by stock value
    Print results

Termination:
    Print item count and total stock value
    Add 1 to lines printed counter
    Print termination message

> Heading:
>   If page count greater than 0 eject a page
>   Add 1 to page counter
>   Print headings
>   Set line counter to number of lines printed

Enhanced Basic Program for Page Breaks

```
' Program    : CH6EX1.BAS
' Programmer : Kristin Higgins
' Date       : June 14, 1990
' Data File  : CH6EX1.DAT
' Purpose    : To read records from the sports inventory file
'            : and print a report listing the value of the
'            : stock. Program generates page breaks.
'
' Mainline
' ~~~~~~~~
  gosub init
  do until eof(1)
     gosub process
  loop
  gosub terminate
  end

' Init Routine
' ~~~~~~~~~~~~
init:

  open "CH6EX1.DAT" for input as #1

  h1$ = "\           \      SPORTS EXMPORIUM STOCK REPORT    Page: ##"
  h2$ = "ITEM              QUANTITY            ITEM            STOCK"
  h3$ = "NAME              ON  HAND            COST            VALUE"
  d1$ = "\           \      ##,###         #####,.##      ########,.##"
  t1$ = "Number of Items   :    ###,###"
  t2$ = "Total Stock Value : $$########,.##"
  item.count = 0
  total.stock.value = 0
  page.count = 0
  gosub headings                    'print headings on first page
  return

' Process Routine
' ~~~~~~~~~~~~~~~
process:

  input #1, item.name$, qty.on.hand, item.cost
  if line.count >= 55 then gosub headings   'check page full
  stock.value = qty.on.hand * item.cost
  lprint  using d1$; item.name$, qty.on.hand, item.cost, stock.value
  line.count = line.count + 1
  item.count = item.count + 1
  total.stock.value = total.stock.value + stock.value
  return

' Terminate Routine
' ~~~~~~~~~~~~~~~~~
terminate:

  lprint
  lprint using t1$; item.count
  lprint using t2$; total.stock.value
  return
```

```
' Headings  Routine
' ~~~~~~~~~~~~~~~~~~

headings:

   if page.count > 0 then lprint chr$(12)   'page eject if not first
   page.count = page.count + 1
   lprint
   lprint
   lprint using h1$; date$, page.count
   lprint
   lprint h2$
   lprint h3$
   lprint
   line.count = 7
   return

' End of Program File
' ~~~~~~~~~~~~~~~~~~~
```

Output from CH6EX1.BAS

```
06-18-1991        SPORTS EXMPORIUM STOCK REPORT      Page:   1

ITEM              QUANTITY            ITEM              STOCK
NAME              ON   HAND           COST              VALUE

Hockey Stick           23             18.75            431.25
Badminton Net          11              5.75             63.25

Number of Items  :          2
Total Stock Value :     $494.50
```

Review Questions

1. Write the pseudocode for the heading routine.

2. Which routines call (GOSUB) the heading routine?

3. In which routine would you include the statement(s) to set up the edit masks for the heading lines?

4. What is the basic statement to check for page full, and which routine would this statement be coded in?

5. In which routine(s) would you increment the line counter?

6. In which routine(s) would you reset the line counter?

Programming Problems:

Problem #1 - Service Charge Report

INSTRUCTIONS:

The customer account system at ABC Company Limited is to be enhanced to include a program to calculate the service charge for all customer accounts and print a report in the format shown below.

INPUT:

Input is from a file called CUST.DAT. The record layout will be as follows:

customer number   - 4 digits

customer name   - maximum 20 characters

balance due   - $$$$.cc

OUTPUT

The company assesses a monthly service charge of 1.5% on the first $500.00 of the balance due, plus 1% on any additional balance above $500.00.

The output is to be edited as shown on the sample report. Consider that the data file is large and will span pages. Print the current system date and page number in the title line. At the end of the report print totals for balance due, service charge, and total due.

```
1-01-92            SERVICE CHARGE REPORT         PAGE: 1
                    CUSTOMER ACCOUNT SYSTEM


   CUSTOMER  CUSTOMER         BALANCE      SERVICE      TOTAL
   NUMBER    NAME             DUE          CHARGE       DUE
     5677    McDonalds        1,345.66     15.96        1,361.62
     0876    Pastas Pizza       567.99      8.18          576.17
     5647    Lubners Deli        56.98      0.85           57.83
     0073    Moe Lester           9.32      0.14            9.46
     2690    Frank Futher        67.21      1.01           68.22
     4554    Richard Updight    897.77     11.48          909.25

     TOTAL                    2,944.93     37.62       $2,982.55
```

Problem #2 - Inventory Valuation Report

INSTRUCTIONS:

The Seal-O-Tite Gasket Company manufactures rubber gaskets for the construction industry. Their inventory consists of rubber gasket material of varying shapes (styles) stored on reels, with the unit of measurement as feet.

INPUT:

The inventory data are stored in a file called INVMST.DAT, which has the following fields and types of data.

Field	Data	Units
Inventory Number	9999AA99	
Style	AAAAAAAA	
Beginning Balance	99999	ft.
Sold	99999	ft.
Received	99999	ft.
Scrapped	99999	ft.
Feet per Pound	99.9999	ft./lb.
Cost per Pound	99.9999	$./lb.

The field Beginning Balance represents the actual inventory count that is made every three months (end of a quarter year). The other fields are changed as stock is received, sold or scrapped during the next quarter.

OUTPUT:

The current inventory balance can be calculated by using the relation:

Current Balance = Beginning balance + Received - Sold - Scrap

The inventory value can then be calculated by converting the current balance in feet into pounds, using the feet per pound field, and then multiplying the pounds by cost per pound. Consider that the report will span pages. A sample format of the program output is shown below:

```
01-01-92              Seal-O-Tite Gasket Co.              Page: 1
                      Inventory Valuation Report
_____

Inventory        Beginning                         Closing   Inventory
Number    Style  Balance Received Sold  Scrap      Balance   Value

1010AC52  12345678  99,999  99,999  99,999  99,999  99,999  $99,999.99
1010AC52  12345678  99,999  99,999  99,999  99,999  99,999  $99,999.99
1010AC52  12345678  99,999  99,999  99,999  99,999  99,999  $99,999.99
1010AC52  12345678  99,999  99,999  99,999  99,999  99,999  $99,999.99
1010AC52  12345678  99,999  99,999  99,999  99,999  99,999  $99,999.99

              Inventory Total Value               $9,999,999.99
_____
```

CHAPTER 7

Advanced Variable Types

Advanced Variable Types	93
Numeric Types	93
Why Use Different Variable Types	95
Arithmetic and Data Types	96
Integer Arithmetic Operators	96
Integer Division	96
Practical Application of Integer Arithmetic	97
Review Questions	98

Advanced Variable Types

Until now we have recognized only two types of data:

String

> string literals in quotes (i.e., "hello")
> string variables designated by a $ at the end of the variable name
> (i.e., SURNAME$)

Numeric

> numeric - constants (i.e., 43)
> numeric variables (i.e., STOCK.VALUE)

There are more than two types of data. Numeric data can be subdivided into **three** more specific types.

Numeric Types

Integers:

- whole numbers (i.e., no decimal positions)

- in the range of -32,768 to +32,767

- occupy 2 bytes of memory

- variables identified with a trailing % sign
  sample: COUNT%, PIECES%

Single Precision

- numbers that may have a decimal point

- consist of up to 7 significant digits (trailing and leading zeroes do not count as significant digits)

    sample:
    123.456 has 6 significant digits
    .000123456 has 6 significant digits
    1000000000 has 1 significant digit
    1000001 has 7 significant digits

- occupy 4 bytes of memory

- default numeric variable type (i.e. no trailing symbol) or variables identified with a trailing ! sign

    sample:
    STOCK.VALUE
    FINAL.TOTAL!

Double Precision

- numbers that may have a decimal point

- consist of up to 17 significant digits

    sample:
    123456.78

- occupy 8 bytes of memory

- variables identified with a trailing # sign

    sample:
    LARGE.TOTAL#
    STOCK.VALUE#

As seen above, the type of a numeric variable is designated by the suffix character included in the variable name. If no suffix character is provided, the default of single precision is assumed. Therefore, all of the numeric variables you have been using to this point have been single precision by default.

The suffix character included at the end of a variable name is part of the actual variable name. Therefore, the variable STOCK.VALUE and STOCK.VALUE# are two unique and separate variables in memory. The variable STOCK.VALUE and STOCK.VALUE! are, however, the same variable, as the ! sign is the default single precision. Programmers must therefore be particularly careful to ensure that the correct variable name is always provided, complete with the suffix character ($, %, #) desired.

Why Use Different Variable Types

1. It is obvious that the programmer must use string variables to store character data.

2. If your program includes a variable for a value such as line counter, decimal positions would not be required, and the value would not exceed 32,767. The programmer may wish to store the counter in an integer variable (i.e., LINE.COUNT%) to save 2 bytes of main memory (the difference between single precision at 4 bytes, and integer at 2 bytes). Being frugal in the use of main memory was common in the past, when main memory was expensive and many computers had only a small amount of main memory. Today main memory is cheap, and computers have plenty. Using an integer variable to save 2 bytes of main memory is not worth the risk and trouble it takes to be careful that the % suffix on the variable name is consistently used.

3. If you recognize that the value stored in a variable may possibly exceed 7 significant digits, then it is necessary to use a double precision variable. It is always wise to err on the side of safety and choose double precision, even if there is only a remote chance during even a future run, that the value will exceed 7 significant digits. If a double precision variable is not used for values exceeding 7 significant digits, then the value will be rounded to fit in the available memory, effectively loosing accuracy in the value.

4. Numeric variable types affect certain arithmetic calculations, as discussed next. A programmer may wish to make use of these arithmetic features by specifying a particular type.

Arithmetic and Data Types

Storing values with decimal positions into integer variables will cause the value to be rounded to the nearest whole number before it is stored.

     Sample
A% = 11 / 4   A%   will contain the value 3, which is 2.75 rounded
A% = 9 / 4   A%   will contain the value 2, which is 2.25 rounded
A! = 11 / 4   A!   will contain 2.75
A = 11 / 4   A   will contain 2.75 (same as above)

Integer Arithmetic Operators

In addition to the arithmetic operators already discussed (i.e., + - * /), there are two operators that are termed integer operators, because they only return whole numbers.

Integer Division

The use of a \ (backslash) instead of the standard / (slash) for division affects the calculated result. Integer division produces a truncated quotient with no remainder.

     Sample:
A = 9 \ 4   A will contain 2 (the number of times 4 is divisible evenly into 9)
A = 11 \ 4   A will again contain 2 (the number of times 4 is divisible evenly into 11)

MOD Operator

The remainder of an integer division can be obtained by using the MOD (modulo) operator. The MOD operator is like the integer division operator, except that it returns the remainder instead of the quotient.

     Sample:
A = 9 MOD 4   A will contain 1, the remainder
A = 11 MOD 4   A will contain 3, the remainder

Practical Application of Integer Arithmetic

A common application of integer arithmetic is in converting a total time in minutes, to the number of hours and minutes (e.g., 200 minutes is 3 hours and 20 minutes)

The variable TOTAL.MINUTES contains the total minutes. The code to calculate the hours and store it in the variable HOURS, and minutes in MINUTES would be:

```
HOURS = TOTAL.MINUTES \ 60
MINUTES = TOTAL.MINUTES MOD 60
```

Review Questions

1. List each variable type and indicate the associated suffix character, and number of bytes each would occupy in memory.

2. Identify the type of numeric precision for each of the following values.

   12   1.45   0.0000000243   1.0000000243   30000   40000

3. Would it be possible to include both the variables QTY and QTY$ in the same program? Explain.

4. Indicate the value of the target variable (i.e. a*) after each of the given statements, assuming

   i) that the variable b contains the value 7.

   ii) that the variable b contains the value 8.

   ```
   a = b / 3              a% = b / 3
   a! = b / 3             a# = b / 3
   a% = b \ 3             a = b \ 3
   a = b MOD 3
   ```

5. CHANGE CONVERTER

Write a program that will accept monetary values of amount owed to a customer from an input file, and covert it into the appropriate number of bills and coins of each denomination required to generate that particular amount owing. Assume the following denominations are available: penny, nickel, dime, quarter, loonie, $2 bill, $5 bill, $10 bill, $20 bill, $100 bill.

e.g., $147.89

1 x $100, 2 x $20, 1 x $5, 1 x $2, 3 x quarter, 1 x dime, 4 x penny

CHAPTER 8

Group Totals

Group Totals	**100**
Data File Organization	**101**
Detecting Control Breaks	**102**
Group Totals	**103**
Report Total – Sum of Sum Logic	**104**
First Attempt at Pseudocode for Program With Group Totals	**105**
Logic Omissions	**107**
False Control Break at the Start	**107**
Missing Last Group Total Display	**108**
Correct Pseudocode for Group Total Logic	**109**
Group Totals Program	**110**
Review Questions	**111**

Group Totals

A common feature of business reports is to provide subtotals of groups of data throughout the report. An example of subtotals can be seen in the following weekly payroll report. The data file would contain one record for each period of work performed by every employee during the week. If the company had 40 employees, each working 5 days a week, the minimum size of the data file for 1 week would therefore be 200 records (5 * 40). The task of the program would be to print a report displaying each work record, with a weekly subtotal for every employee. These subtotals are commonly referred to as **group totals**. The output would appears as follows:

```
10-07-1990              Widget Company Ltd.            Page:   1
                           Weekly Payroll

Employee              Date               Hours                 Gross
Number                                   Worked                  Pay
  112               10/01/90               8                   84.00
  112               10/02/90               8                   84.00
  112               10/03/90               3                   22.50
  112               10/03/90               6                   63.00
                                  Employee Total            $253.50*

  171               10/01/90               8                   79.60
  171               10/02/90               6                   59.70
  171               10/03/90               8                   63.75
  171               10/03/90               4                   48.00
  171               10/04/90               8                   79.60
  171               10/05/90               8                   79.60
                                  Employee Total            $410.25*

  189               10/01/90               9                   54.00
  189               10/03/90               8                   60.00
  189               10/04/90               8                   84.00
  189               10/05/90               8                  100.00
  189               10/06/90               8                   60.00
                                  Employee Total            $358.00*

                                     Grand Total          $1,021.75**
```

Data File Organization

Each data record in the file would contain 4 fields; employee number, date worked, hours worked, and rate of pay on that task. Each employee would have multiple records in the data file, one for each task performed in the week. If the records for a given employee were scattered throughout the data file, creating the above report would be very difficult. Remember that each record must be read **in order** in a sequential data file. For a program to produce subtotals for an employee, the entire data file would have be processed, selecting only the records for that employee. This procedure would have to be repeated, processing the whole file once for every employee.

If the data file was organized differently, subtotals could be produced with only **one** pass through the data. The records in the data file would have to be arranged in sorted order, such that all records for one employee were together. If records in the data file were arranged in this sequence before processing the data, then totals for each employee could be generated easily. For the payroll report, the records in the data file would be sequenced in ascending order of employee number, thus effectively grouping all of the records for one employee together.

In data processing this concept of data organization and group totals is described using specific terminology.

Control Field: The field in the data file used to arrange the records.

Control Group: All the data records with identical values in the control field.

Control Break: The "breaking point" in data processing between one control group, and the next control group.

Group Total: The total of desired values for one control group.

The following is the data file that was used to create the payroll report. Notice that it is sorted in ascending order by the control field **employee number**.

Detecting Control Breaks

Data for Control Break Example

```
112 , "10/01/90" , 8   , 10.5
112 , "10/02/90" , 8   , 10.5
112 , "10/03/90" , 3   , 7.5
112 , "10/03/90" , 6   , 10.5
171 , "10/01/90" , 8   , 9.95
171 , "10/02/90" , 6   , 9.95
171 , "10/03/90" , 7.5 , 8.50
171 , "10/03/90" , 4   , 12
171 , "10/04/90" , 8   , 9.95
171 , "10/05/90" , 8   , 9.95
189 , "10/01/90" , 9   , 6.00
189 , "10/03/90" , 8   , 7.50
189 , "10/04/90" , 8   , 10.5
189 , "10/05/90" , 8   , 12.5
189 , "10/06/90" , 8   , 7.5
```

For most of the program, the logic is similar to a program without group totals. Each record is input, processed, and displayed in the PROCESS routine. The only twist is that group totals must be displayed after all the records for one control group have been processed, and before the first record in the next control group is processed.

Look at the data file. At what point would you print the total for the employee? It is quite obvious to a human looking at the entire data file at which point group totals would be printed. Remember, however, that the computer only processes one record at a time. It can not "peek" ahead in the data file to determine if the next record belongs to a new control group. Pretend that you are the computer and process the data file as a program would, revealing only one record at a time. As each record is revealed ask yourself, "Is it time for a group total?". You quickly realize that it is not until the first record of a new control group is read that you know it is time to print the total of the last control group.

Even this manual exercise does not clearly indicate the nature of the problem of detecting control breaks. When revealing one record at a time, you probably allowed yourself to **look back** to the previous record, to compare the value in the control field just read to the previous record's control field. If you were to truly mimic the actions of the program, then you would only

Chapter 8 Group Totals 103

reveal one record at time, covering up all the previous and subsequent records.

The computer can not perform this "looking-back" action in the PROCESS routine as we know it. At the start of each pass through the process routine, a data record is input into memory variables. When the data record is input into memory variables, it "knocks out" the values from the previous data record in those variables. Therefore we have a problem comparing the current record to the previous record, as the program has no recollection of the previous record.

The action of comparing the current value of the control field to the previous value could be accomplished if the value was **saved** to another variable before the next record was input. This would require a new memory variable to store (save) the value of current control field before the next record is input.

This is exactly the action required in program logic to allow group totals. In the PROCESS routine, the data record is input, and the current value in the control field is compared with the saved value to see if they are different (if so a group total should be displayed), then the current value is assigned to the save variable, effectively saving it before the next pass through the PROCESS routine.

Group Totals

Logic for group totals is not much different from logic for report totals. The value of the group total is increased by the value of the current record, at each pass through the PROCESS routine. The only difference is that when a control break is detected, the current value of the group total variable is displayed, **and** the group total variable is then reset to 0 to begin accumulating anew for the next group.

Remembering that the program must also handle page breaks. There are three actions to be performed whenever a control break is detected. Following the Top Down Design approach, these actions are best combined into a separate subroutine to handle group total printing.

GROUPTOTAL Routine

    print the group total

    increment the line counter by the number of lines printed for the group total (include blank lines too)

    set the group total back to zero

Report Totals – Sum of Sum Logic

Report totals (also referred to as Final or Grand totals) appear at the end of a report. In a program that produces group totals and a final total, separate variables must be established for the group total and the final total. The logic to produce final totals has been covered in previous chapters. As a review of totaling, the value for each record is added to the final total variable in the PROCESS routine, which is repeated for each record. The final total is printed in the TERMINATION routine, which is performed one time only at the end of processing. This procedure can, however, be **optimized** in a program that produces group totals.

To detect the optimization, use a calculator to accumulate the final total of the output displayed at the start of the chapter, in the quickest way possible.

If you added up the value of each employee's individual records, it took 15 additions to calculate the final total. This is one way a program can calculate final totals, and indeed is how our programs have calculated them to this point.

If you added up the value of each employee's group total, then it only took three additions to calculate the final total; a definite optimization. This technique is call "sum of sums" since the final total (sum) is calculated by adding group totals (sums).

This optimization could be incorporated into the program logic of a group total program, thus saving the computer run time. It involves two changes to existing program logic. Instead of adding individual record values to the final total, **add the group total to the final total**. The group total should be added to the final total only when a control break is detected, not each time a record is processed. This means removing the final total accumulation from the PROCESS routine, which is repeated for each record, and placing it **in the new GROUPTOTAL routine,** which is repeated each time a control break is detected. Now the new GROUPTOTAL routine contains four actions. Note that the value of the final total would still be printed in the TERMINATE routine, when all processing is complete.

First Attempt at Pseudocode for Program with Group Totals

The following pseudocode depicts the changes in standard report program logic, to accomplish group totals. The additions are highlighted.

VTOC:

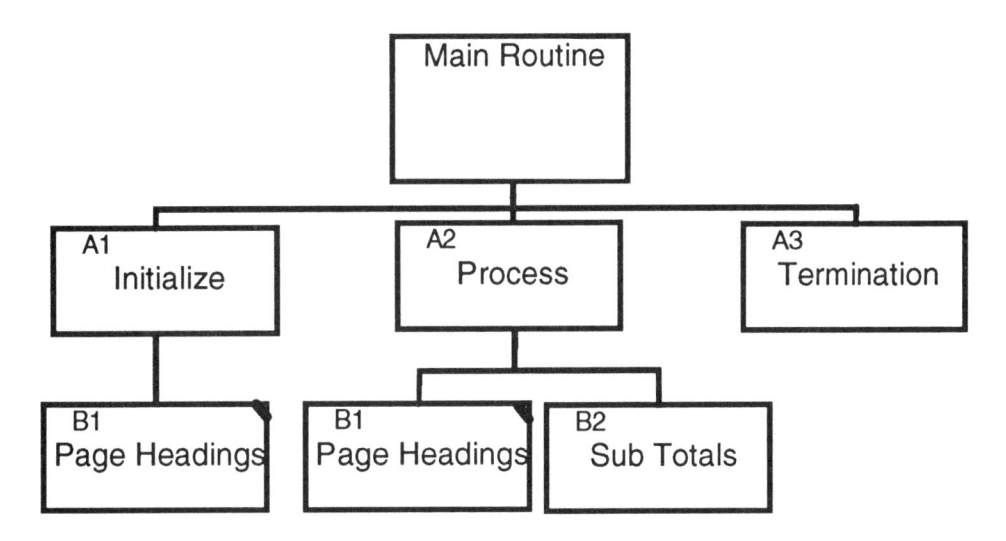

```
                    Main Routine
          ┌─────────────┼─────────────┐
        A1            A2            A3
     Initialize      Process      Termination
          │           ┌─┴─┐
         B1          B1   B2
    Page Headings  Page  Sub Totals
                  Headings
```

Pseudocode

Mainline:

    Perform Initialization Routine

    Perform the Process Routine repeatedly until there are no more data records

    Perform the Termination Routine

Initialization:

    Open the data file

    Setup headings and edit masks

    Initialize line counter and page counter to 0

    Initialize group total and final total to 0

    Perform Heading Routine

Process:

    Read data record

    If employee number not same as save employee number

        perform GroupTotal routine

    Set the save employee number to employee

    Routine

    Compute gross pay = hours worked * rate of pay

    Increase employee total pay by gross pay

    Print detail line

    Increase line count

Termination:

    Print final total pay

    Heading:Print employee total pay

    Add employee total pay to final total pay

    Set employee total pay to 0

Increase line count

    Eject page

    Add 1 to page count

    Print Headings

    Set line counter to number of heading lines printed

Grouptotal:

    Print employee total pay

    Add employee total pay to final total pay

    Set employee total to 0

    Increase line count

Logic Omissions

If the logic of the preceding pseudocode was followed the following output would be generated. Can you spot the problem areas?

False Control Break at the Start

```
10-07-1990              Widget Company Ltd.              Page:  1
                           Weekly Payroll

Employee           Date              Hours                   Gross
Number                               Worked                  Pay


                                  Employee Total           $0.00*
  112            10/01/90               8                   84.00
  112            10/02/90               8                   84.00
  112            10/03/90               3                   22.50
  112            10/03/90               6                   63.00
                                  Employee Total         $253.50*
  171            10/01/90               8                   79.60
  171            10/02/90               6                   59.70
  171            10/03/90               8                   63.75
  171            10/03/90               4                   48.00
  171            10/04/90               8                   79.60
  171            10/05/90               8                   79.60
                                  Employee Total         $410.25*
  189            10/01/90               9                   54.00
  189            10/03/90               8                   60.00
  189            10/04/90               8                   84.00
  189            10/05/90               8                  100.00
  189            10/06/90               8                   60.00
                                   Grand Total           $663.75**
```

Why did a group total appear before any detail lines on the report? In order to answer this, remember what a variable contains when the program starts running. Suppose the programmer has chosen to the store the employee number in a string variable, and similarly the save variable for the last employee number would also be a string variable. Initial contents of a string variable is **null**.

After the INPUT statement is executed in the first pass through the process routine, the employee number variable will contain the first employee number in the data file (i.e., 112). The save employee number variable will still contain **null**. When the contents of these two variables are compared they are not equal, causing the GROUPTOTAL subroutine to be executed.

The control break logic must be amended to detect a control break when the value of the control field is not the same as the saved value **and** it is not the first record (i.e., first pass through the PROCESS routine). The program would be able to recognize the first pass through the PROCESS routine, because at this point the contents of the save variable will still be null.

Missing Last Group Total Display

Upon closer examination of the erroneous output, it is evident that the last group's total is not displayed, nor is it included in the final total.

This occurred because there is no logic in the pseudocode to **flush** out the last group total. The process routine is executed for the last record, and immediately after that the TERMINATION routine is executed.

Logic could be amended to display the last group total, and add it to the final total before the final total is printed. Since the action of printing the group total, and adding it to the final total is accomplished in the GROUPTOTAL routine, the pseudocode could be fixed by inserting:

    Perform Grouptotal Routine

as the first action in the TERMINATE routine.

Revised VTOC:

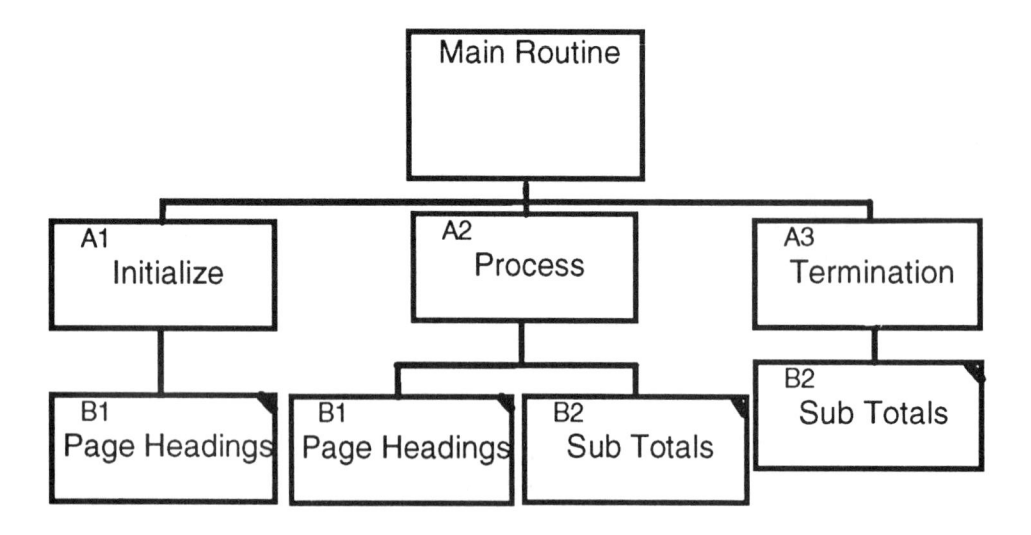

```
                    Main Routine
         ┌──────────────┼──────────────┐
    A1              A2              A3
  Initialize       Process        Termination
      │         ┌────┴────┐            │
    B1         B1         B2          B2
Page Headings Page Headings Sub Totals Sub Totals
```

Correct Pseudocode for Group Total Logic

Mainline:

    Perform Initialization Routine

    Perform the Process Routine repeatedly until there are no more data records

    Perform the Termination Routine

Initialization:

    Open the data file

    Setup headings and edit masks

    Initialize line counter and page counter to 0

    Initialize group total and final total to 0

    Initialize save employee number to null

    Perform Heading Routine

Process:

    Read data record

    If employee number not same as save employee number
        and save employee number not null

        perform GroupTotal routine

    Set the save employee number to employee

    If line count exceeds maximum lines per page perform Heading Routine

    Compute gross pay = hours worked * rate of pay

    Increase employee total pay by gross pay

    Print detail line

    Increase line count

Termination:

    Perform Grouptotal routine

    Print final total pay

Heading

    Eject page

    Add 1 to page count

    Print Headings

    Set line counter to number of heading lines printed

Grouptotal:

    Print employee total pay

    Add employee total pay to final total pay

    Set employee total pay to 0

    Increase line count

Group Totals Program

```
'   Program      : CH8EX1A.BAS
'   Programmer   : Kristin Higgins
'   Date         : Jun 12, 1990
'   Data File    : CH8EX1.DAT
'   Purpose      : To read records from a weekly employee work file that
'                : is sorted by employee number, and create a report
'                : listing individual work records, and total pay for each
'                : employee.
'                : Report had group totals.
'
'   Mainline
'   ~~~~~~~~
    gosub init
    do until eof(1)
       gosub process
    loop
    gosub terminate
    end

'   Init Routine
'   ~~~~~~~~~~~~
init:
    open "a:CH8EX1.DAT" for input as #1
    h1$ = "\            \                Widget Company Ltd_.             Page: ##"
    h2$ = "                                Weekly Payroll"
    h3$ = "Employee           Date              Hours                  Gross"
    h4$ = "Number                             Worked                    Pay"
    d1$ = "  \   \          \       \           ####              #######,.##"
    t1$ = "                                 Employee Total     $$#######,.## *"
    t2$ = "                                 Grand Total        $$#######,.##_*_*"
    line.count = 0
    page.count = 0
    employee.total = 0
    grand.total = 0
    save.emp.num$ = ""
    gosub heading
    return

'   Process Routine
'   ~~~~~~~~~~~~~~~
Process:
    input #1, emp.num$, work.date$, hours.worked, rate.of.pay
    if emp.num$ <> save.emp.num$ and save.emp.num$ <> "" then gosub grouptotal
    save.emp.num$ = emp.num$
    if line.count >= 55 then gosub heading
    gross.pay = hours.worked * rate.of.pay
    employee.total = employee.total + gross.pay
    lprint using d1$; emp.num$, work.date$, hours.worked, gross.pay
    line.count = line.count + 1
    return

'   Terminate Routine
'   ~~~~~~~~~~~~~~~~~
Terminate:
    gosub grouptotal
    lprint using t2$; grand.total
    return


'   Heading Routine
'   ~~~~~~~~~~~~~~~
Heading:
    if page.count > 0 then lprint chr$(12)
    page.count = page.count + 1
    lprint
    lprint
    lprint using h1$; date$, page.count
    lprint h2$
    lprint
    lprint h3$
    lprint h4$
    lprint
    line.count = 9
    return

'   Grouptotal Routine
'   ~~~~~~~~~~~~~~~~~~
Grouptotal:
    lprint
    lprint using t1$; employee.total
    lprint
    grand.total = grand.total + employee.total
    employee.total = 0
    line.count = line.count + 3
    return
```

Review Questions

Problem #1 – Store Inventory Report

INSTRUCTIONS:

Design and code a BASIC program to produce an inventory report for a store, with subtotals by department.

INPUT:

Input is from the sequential file STOREINV.DAT. Each record in the file will contain department number, item code, quantity on hand, and item cost per unit. The file will be sorted by department number. Examine the file before beginning, to ascertain the maximum size of each of the fields.

OUTPUT:

Output is a printed inventory report for the store, listing department number, item code, quantity on hand, cost, and the total value. On a change of department number, display a total for that department. After all records have been processed, a summary is to be displayed which lists the grand total value. Note: be careful to handle page breaks correctly. Following is a sample of how the output should appear. This is just a sample report and does not contain all the data in the file STOREINV.DAT.

```
   06-11-1992        SUPER STORES OF CANADA INC.      PAGE  1
                          INVENTORY REPORT

   DEPARTMENT        ITEM      QTY ON       COST        TOTAL
   NUMBER            CODE      HAND

      0100           AB34         7         15.25       106.75
      0100           AB37         1          7.78         7.78
      0100           MB35        16          9.98       159.68
      0100           NB01       100          4.40       440.00
      0100           QR24        15          6.74       101.10
                            DEPARTMENT 0100 TOTAL     $815.31*
      0200           WC31         5         50.00       250.00
      0200           NA26        16          2.85        45.60
      0200           RL96         3         12.34        37.02
                            DEPARTMENT 0200 TOTAL     $332.62*
      0300           HL94        11          6.38        70.18
      0300           GJ49         4          5.38        21.52
      0300           FO80        44          0.98        43.12
      0300           ME73         6         33.67       202.02
      0300           JV77         2         38.60        77.20
      0300           KL11         1        321.00       321.00
                            DEPARTMENT 0300 TOTAL     $735.04*
                                     GRAND TOTAL    $1,882.97**
```

Problem #2 – A Fees Report for Student Enrollment

INSTRUCTIONS:

Design and code a BASIC program to produce a fees report for a school with subtotals by student.

INPUT:

Input is from the sequential file STUDENT.DAT. Each record in the file will contain student number, course number, and charge code. The charge code will be the letter A, B or C. The file will be sorted by student number. Examine the file before beginning, to ascertain the maximum size of each of the fields.

OUTPUT:

Output is a printed enrollment report for the school, listing student number, course number and fees. The fees are calculated based on the charge code as follows: A - 78.50, B - 88.50, C - 125.99. On a change of student number, print a total for that student. After all records have been processed, a summary is to be printed, which lists the grand total fees. Note: be careful to handle page breaks correctly. Following is a sample of how the output should appear. This is just a sample report and does not contain all the data in the file STUDENT.DAT.

```
    06-11-1992        DISTRICT NIGHT SCHOOL       PAGE   1
                        ENROLLMENT REPORT

    STUDENT           COURSE          CHARGE             FEES
    NUMBER            NUMBER          CODE

    01293458          220321            A                78.50
    01293458          530311            B                88.50
    01293458          620351            A                78.50
    01293458          813124            C               125.99

                      STUDENT 01293458 TOTAL          $371.49*

    01112233          220321            B                88.50
    01112233          442611            B                88.50
    01112233          932351            A                78.50

                      STUDENT 01112233 TOTAL          $255.50*

                             GRAND TOTAL             $626.99**
```

Problem #3 – Service Centre Report

INSTRUCTIONS:

A sales report for a service centre is to be prepared. Design and code a BASIC program to produce the report.

INPUT:

Input is from the sequential file CLUNKER.DAT. Each record in the file will contain customer number, licence number, charge code, description of work, and amount charged. The charge code will be the letter "L" for labour, and "P" for parts. The file will be sorted on licence number within customer number. Examine the file before beginning, to ascertain the maximum size of each of the fields.

OUTPUT:

Output is a printed sales report for the month, listing customer number, licence number, charge code (L or P), description of work and amount charged. On a change of customer number, print a total of all charges for that customer. After all records have been processed, a sales summary is to be printed, which lists the total monthly sales. Note: be careful to handle page breaks correctly. Attached is a sample of how the output should appear. This is just a sample report and does not contain all the data in the file CLUNKER.DAT.

```
10-24-1991                FAST AUTO SUPPLIES                PAGE  1
                          MONTHLY SALES REPORT

CUSTOMER     LICENCE     CODE    DESCRIPTION                  CHARGE

  0153       HOE 392      P      WIPERS                         6.42
  0153       HOE 392      L      BREAKS INSPECTION             42.53
  0153       HOE 392      L      BREAKS OVERHAUL AND REPAIR   264.66
  0153       HOE 392      P      DRUMS LININGS PADS           345.50
  0153       OME 491      L      OIL CHANGE                     4.27
  0153       OME 491      L      TUNE UP                       34.60
  0153       OME 491      P      PLUGS WIRES AND BELTS         59.30
  0153       OME 491      P      OIL                            8.99

                                      CUSTOMER  0153  TOTAL    $766.27*

  3321       ABX 382      L      BATTERY INSTALLATION          10.40
  3321       ABX 382      P      LIFE TIME BATTERY             84.90

                                      CUSTOMER  3321  TOTAL     $95.30*

  5001       DOT 193      L      INSTALLATION - HEAD LIGHT     17.60
  5001       DOT 193      P      HEAD LIGHT                    21.43
  5001       WNX 445      L      TRANSMISSION LABOUR          310.13
  5001       WNX 445      P      TRANSMISSION                 204.00

                                      CUSTOMER  5001  TOTAL    $553.16*

                                         GRAND TOTAL SALES   $1,414.73**
```

ENHANCEMENTS

1. Modify your program to display the full word PARTS when the charge code is P, and the full word LABOUR when the charge code is L.

2. In the summary report at the end of the report, show summary totals of the sales as split into LABOUR and PARTS.

ADVANCED ENHANCEMENTS

3. Enhance your program to include two levels of control breaks. Include a control break for licence number within customer number. (Notice that the car with licence XCT 499 changed ownership from customer 7215 to customer 7800. Your report should handle this correctly!)

Problem #4 – Payroll Report

INSTRUCTIONS:

A weekly payroll report for a manufacturing company is to be prepared. Design and code a BASIC program to produce the report.

INPUT:

Input is from the sequential file EMPLOYEE.DAT. Each record in the file will contain employee number, day of week (i.e., 1 to 7), hours worked, labour code and earnings. The labour code will contain the letter "P" for production, and "M" for maintenance. The file will be sorted on day of week within employee number. Examine the file before beginning, to ascertain the maximum size of each of the fields.

OUTPUT:

Output is a printed payroll analysis report for the week, listing employee number, day of week, labour code, hours worked and earnings. On a change of employee number, print a total of all earnings for that employee. After all records have been processed, a payroll summary is to be printed, which lists the total weekly earnings. Note: be careful to handle page breaks correctly. Following is a sample of how the output should appear. This is just a sample report and does not contain all the data in the file EMPLOYEE.DAT.

```
06-11-1992        ABC WIDGET MANUFACTURING           PAGE   1
                     WEEKLY PAYROLL REPORT

EMPLOYEE          DAY       LABOUR      HOURS        EARNINGS
 NUMBER         OF WEEK      CODE       WORKED

  1032             1           P         8.00         153.12
  1032             2           P         3.25          72.12
  1032             2           M         1.00          15.32
  1032             2           P         6.00         163.10
  1032             5           P         4.50          88.32
  1032             5           M         4.00          60.00

                          EMPLOYEE  1032  TOTAL      $551.98*

  1083             2           P        10.00         263.70
  1083             3           P         4.75         103.40
  1083             3           M         4.00          78.32

                          EMPLOYEE  1083  TOTAL      $445.42*

  2030             3           P         6.00         143.50
  2030             3           M         1.00          15.32

                          EMPLOYEE  2030  TOTAL      $158.82*

                         GRAND  TOTAL  EARNINGS     $1,156.22**
```

ENHANCEMENTS

1. Modify your program to display the full word MAINTENANCE when the labour code is M, and the full word PRODUCTION when the labour code is P.

2. At the end of the report code, show summary totals of the sales as split into PRODUCTION and MAINTENANCE.

ADVANCED ENHANCEMENTS

3. Enhance your program to include two levels of control breaks. Include a control break for day within employee number.

```
06-11-1992        ABC WIDGET MANUFACTURING              PAGE   1
                  WEEKLY PAYROLL REPORT

EMPLOYEE          DAY         LABOUR         HOURS      EARNINGS
 NUMBER         OF WEEK        CODE          WORKED

  1032             1         PRODUCTION       8.00        153.12

                                      DAY 1 TOTAL      $153.12*

  1032             2         PRODUCTION       3.25         72.12
  1032             2         PRODUCTION       7.00        163.10

                                      DAY 2 TOTAL      $235.22*

  1032             5         PRODUCTION       4.50         88.32
  1032             5         MAINTENANCE      4.00         60.00

                                      DAY 5 TOTAL      $148.32*

                               EMPLOYEE 1032 TOTAL     $536.66**

  1083             2         PRODUCTION      10.00        263.70

                                      DAY 2 TOTAL      $263.70*

  1083             3         PRODUCTION       4.75        103.40
  1083             3         MAINTENANCE      4.00         78.32

                                      DAY 3 TOTAL      $181.72*

                               EMPLOYEE 1083 TOTAL     $445.42**

  2030             3         PRODUCTION       6.00        143.50
  2030             3         MAINTENANCE      1.00         15.50

                                      DAY 3 TOTAL      $159.00*

                               EMPLOYEE 2030 TOTAL     $159.00**

                               GRAND TOTAL EARNINGS   $1,141.08***

                           TOTAL MAINTENANCE CHARGES   $153.82
                           TOTAL PRODUCTION  CHARGES   $987.26
```

CHAPTER 9

Repetitive Processing

Repetitive Processing – Looping	118
Controlled Loops	118
DO/ LOOP	118
WHILE/ WEND	120
Counted Loops	120
FOR/ NEXT	121
Nested Loops	123
Summary	123
Review Questions	124

Repetitive Processing – Looping

Repetitive processing involves the repetitive execution of a section of code. This is commonly referred to as looping. A programmer probably does not wish the actions in a loop repeated indefinitely. Looping constructs are therefore designed with control mechanisms, to allow the programmer to dictate in their logic the point at which the repetition should end. The term "controlled loop" is given to a loop in which a programmer can set the *condition* to terminate the execution of the loop.

Controlled Loops

DO / LOOP

We have already examined in brief the DO / LOOP statements. This is one example of the controlled loop constructs available in Basic. The DO / LOOP pair of statements actually has more versatility than previously stated. The generic form of the statement pair is:

```
DO  [{WHILE/UNTIL} condition]
    .
    . body of loop
    .  (statements within the loop typically indented)
    .
[LOOP] [{WHILE/UNTIL} condition]
```

The condition portion of the statement is the same as the logical expression in an IF statement examined earlier. The condition may be stated in the WHILE form, in which case repetition of the loop will continue WHILE THE CONDITION IS TRUE, or in the UNTIL form, in which case the loop will be executed UNTIL THE CONDITION BECOMES TRUE. One is effectively the reverse of the other. The condition may be encoded at the start (as part of the DO statement) or at the end (as part of LOOP statement). Where the condition is encoded affects when the testing is done. If the condition is located at the top of the loop in the DO statement, it is called a pre-test. The condition will be tested at the start of each pass through the loop. If the condition is true the loop will be executed, otherwise execution will jump to the statement after the LOOP statement.

If the programmer does not want the condition tested before the loop is executed the first time, then the condition would be encoded at the end of the loop in the LOOP statement. This is called a post-test condition, as the

Chapter 9   Repetitive Processing   119

condition is not tested until the end of each pass through the loop. The body of a post-test loop is always executed at least once, whereas the body of a pre-test loop may possibly never be executed.

Coding standards dictate that any statements executed conditionally in a program should be indented. The statements in the body of a loop are therefore always indented from the rest of the code.

The following simple programs illustrate the concept of loop control using a DO/LOOP.

PROGRAM	OUTPUT
C = 1	1
DO UNTIL C = 5	2
PRINT C	3
C = C + 1	4
LOOP	DONE LOOP
PRINT "DONE LOOP"	
C = 1	DONE LOOP
DO WHILE C = 5	
PRINT C	
C = C + 1	
LOOP	
PRINT "DONE LOOP"	
C = 1	1
DO	DONE LOOP
PRINT C	
C = C + 1	
LOOP WHILE C = 5	
PRINT "DONE LOOP"	

PROGRAM	OUTPUT
C = 0	1
DO UNTIL C = 5	2
C = C + 1	3
PRINT C	4
LOOP	5
PRINT "DONE LOOP"	DONE LOOP

These programs also illustrate the need to be very precise in the coding of the condition. The same condition was used in the first and fourth loop, but with very different results in execution (notice the output from these loops). Also, the second and third programs contained the same condition. Notice the different output, depending on whether the condition is coded at the start or end of the loop.

There are no hard and fast rules for correct conditions. Each condition depends upon the context in which it is placed and what the programmer wishes to accomplish. Indeed, several conditions will satisfy the same goal, and are merely the same condition stated in different ways.

WHILE / WEND

The WHILE / WEND controlled loop structure is very similar to the DO / LOOP structure. It merely provides the programmer with another means of encoding pre-test loops.

```
WHILE condition
      .
      . body of loop
      .
WEND
```

The condition is always tested at the start of the loop. If it is true, then the loop will be executed. If the condition is false, execution will continue at the statement following the WEND.

Counted Loops

Counted loops differ from controlled loops, in that test for loop control is based on a **built in count,** not a condition. These loops would be used in an application where the programmer knows, before the loop begins, the exact number of times that it should be executed.

As an added benefit, a counted loop has an automatic counter built in. In the previous examples of DO/LOOP execution, a counter was used to best illustrate the condition testing in the loop. The counter control had to be coded separately from the DO statement (i.e., statements were included to initialize the counter and increment it).

FOR/ NEXT

Counted loops are coded using the FOR / NEXT pair of statements in Basic. The general form is:

    FOR counter.variable = start TO stop [STEP increment]

        .

        . body of loop

        .

        NEXT counter.variable

The counter.variable must be a numeric variable. Start, stop and increment may be expressed as a constant, a numeric variable, or an expression. The counter variable must be the same in the FOR statement and the NEXT statement that it is paired with.

Execution of the loop involves several steps.

1. The initial pass through the loop will assign the start value to the counter.variable.

2. The value in the counter variable is compared to the stop value. If it does not exceed the stop value the body of the loop is executed, otherwise execution jumps to the statement following the NEXT statement

3. The NEXT statement causes the counter variable to be increased by the STEP increment (or default of 1 if STEP not specified in the FOR statement).

4. Execution jumps back to the FOR statement at the start of the loop and logic is repeated at step 1 above.

Negative step increments can be used to cause the control variable to count backwards. Decimal values are allowed for start, stop and increment. The control variable may be used in calculations within the loop, but **avoid altering the contents of the control variable within the loop.**

This concept can best be illustrated by sample FOR / NEXT loops.

PROGRAM	OUTPUT
FOR J = 1 TO 5	1
PRINT J	2
NEXT J	3
PRINT "DONE LOOP"	4
	5
	DONE LOOP
FOR K = 1 TO 10 STEP 2	1
PRINT K	3
NEXT K	5
PRINT "DONE LOOP"	7
PRINT "FINAL VALUE OF K IS";K	9
	DONE LOOP
	FINAL VALUE OF K IS 11

What would the output be from the following program?

```
PRINT "THE 4 TIMES TABLE"
PRINT
FOR L = 0 TO 12
    ANSWER = 4 * L
    PRINT "4 x";L;"= ";ANSWER
NEXT L
PRINT "―――――――――."
```

Nested Loops

Any loop construct (DO, WHILE, or FOR) may be nested within another loop. Nesting implies that there is an inner loop *completely* inside of an outer loop. All of the passes through the inner loop will be completed for *each* pass through the outer loop.

This can best be illustrated by a sample of nested FOR / NEXT loops.

PROGRAM	OUTPUT
FOR X = 1 TO 2	OUTER...1
PRINT "OUTER...";X	INNER... 1
FOR Y = 1 TO 3	INNER... 2
PRINT "INNER...";Y	INNER... 3
NEXT Y	OUTER.. 2
NEXT X	INNER... 1
	INNER.. 2
	INNER.. 3

Summary

Many program applications require repetitive processing of a set of actions until a particular condition arises. In the previous chapters, programs have used DO loops to cause the execution of the PROCESS routine to repeat until the end of the data file is reached. In the next chapters, loops will be used in interactive programs to ensure valid data is input by users, and to process arrays.

Which type of loop to use depends on the application. Counted loops are used in the situation where the loop is to be repeated a predetermined number of times. Controlled loops are used in situations where the number of repetitions depends on a condition (e.g., end of file, a data record with sex code of male).

Review Questions

1. Indicate what the output is from the following loops.

   a)
   ```
   x = 0
   DO WHILE x < 5
       PRINT x
       x = x + 1
   LOOP
   ```

   b)
   ```
   x = 0
   DO UNTIL x < 5
       PRINT x
       x = x + 1
   LOOP
   ```

   c)
   ```
   x = 0
   WHILE x < 5
       PRINT x
       x = x + 1
   WEND
   ```

   d)
   ```
   FOR x = 1 TO 10 STEP 3
       PRINT "X IS ";x
   NEXT x
   ```

   e)
   ```
   FOR x = 0 TO 90 STEP 10
       FOR y = 0 TO 9
           ans = x * 10 + y
           PRINT ans
       NEXT y
   NEXT x
   ```

   f)
   ```
   x = 3
   WHILE x > 0
       PRINT x
   WEND
   ```

   g)
   ```
   x = 0
   DO
       PRINT x
       x = x - 1
   LOOP WHILE x > 0
   ```

2. Using a FOR/NEXT loop, write a code segment to create a "2 times" table in the following format.

   ```
   ***** 2 times table *****
   2 x 0 = 0
   2 x 1 = 2
   2 x 2 = 4
     .
     .
   2 x 12 = 24
   ```

3. Using nested FOR/NEXT loops, write a code segment to generate all of the times tables (i.e., one times, two times, ... twelve times), to appear in the same format as indicated in the previous question. Note: each table should appear on a page of its own.

4. a) Write a code segment that will generate the following output, using a FOR/NEXT loop.

   10
   9
   8
   7
   6
   5
   4
   3
   2
   1
   Blastoff!!!!

   b) Now write the code segment, using any looping construct other than FOR/NEXT (i.e. DO or WHILE).

CHAPTER 10

Interactive Programming

Interactive Programming	127
Prompting the User for Input	128
Formatted Screens	129
BASIC Statements for Screen Painting	129
Examples	131
Sample Formatted Screen	132
Program to Paint the Screen	132
Input Editing on a Formatted Screen	133
Pseudocode	134
Discussion of Code	135
Review Questions	136

Interactive Programming

Up to this point, all of the programs that have been developed have obtained input data from a data file. Another common source of input data is the keyboard. Programs that accept input from the keyboard are called **interactive programs,** due to the fact that the program interacts with the user at run time.

Problem:

A teacher requires a program to assist students in calculating their term average. The average is calculated based on three tests.

Test #	Marked out of	Worth
1	25	30%
2	50	30%
3	100	40%

The program should prompt the user for:

student's name

mark on first test

mark on second test

mark on third test

After all marks have been entered, a message should be displayed indicating the student's final percentage in the course.

The program should then prompt the user if she wishes to do another calculation. If the user replies that she does, the process should repeat, otherwise the program should end.

Prompting the User for Input

Until now, values from a data file have been input into variables in main memory, using the INPUT # statement. The file number used in the INPUT # statement indicates that the data will come from a previously opened data file identified by that internal file number.

If no file number is specified in the INPUT statement, then Basic interprets the statement as accepting input from the keyboard, rather than a file.

>Sample:
>
>INPUT   SURNAME$

When Basic executes the above statement, execution will be suspended until the user types a string of characters and presses the enter key. The computer is ultimately patient. It will wait for ever. Once the enter key is pressed, the data typed by the user will be stored in the indicated variable, SURNAME$.

The user must be careful to enter acceptable data. The statement:

>INPUT AGE

requires the user to enter a numeric value. If the user enters a non-numeric value, Basic will detect the error, and treat it as if a zero was entered.

Good interactive programs always give the user a prompt message, to indicate what is to be entered. The prompt may be included as part of the INPUT statement as follows:

>INPUT "What is your age"; AGE

The phrase in quotes will be displayed at the current cursor location on the screen, followed by a question mark and one blank space. The next position on the screen line will contain the flashing cursor indicating that the user may type a response.

If a comma is used instead of a semicolon after the prompt, then the question mark and space will not be displayed at the end of the prompt.

Formatted Screens

Interactive programs can be written to display one prompt at a time, and wait for user input before displaying the next prompt. Another common method of coding interactive programs is to present the user with a formatted screen containing all of the prompts at the start of execution, and positioning the cursor beside each prompt as required.

The second method is preferred since a full screen of prompts gives the user an idea of the entire data required for the process. This is better than the user finding what input is required one item at a time as the prompts appear.

Designing formatted screens can be quite sophisticated depending on how much time effort is put into the screen design. Many programmers refer to this step as "screen painting." In normal video screen size is 80 print positions wide, and 24 lines long. Typical interactive programs reserve the 24th line for error messages.

Basic Statements for Screen Painting

CLS Statement.

Clears the screen to the background colour.

Sample:

```
CLS
```

LOCATE Statement.

Will position the cursor to the specified row (1-24) and column (1-80) on the screen. Row and Col may be numeric constants, numeric variables or expressions.

Sample:

```
LOCATE row,col
```

COLOR Statement

Will set the foreground and background to the specified colours. Foreground and background may be numeric constants, numeric variables or expressions.

Sample:

COLOR foreground, background

Foreground choices:

0	black	8	gray
1	blue	9	light blue
2	green	10	light green
3	cyan	11	light cyan
4	red	12	light red
5	magenta	13	light magenta
6	brown	14	light brown
7	white	15	high intensity white

Background choices:

0 to 6	black background
7	white background

Add 16 to the foreground colour to make the characters "blink."

SPACE$ Function

The SPACE$(n) function returns a string of n spaces. The number of spaces (n) may be specified as a numeric constant, variable or expression.

Sample:

PRINT SPACE$(n)

CHR$ Function

The CHR$(n) will return a one-character string with the ASCII value as specified by (n). Refer to an ASCII chart for the ASCII value of graphics characters to display a box. For example, 218 is the ASCII value of an upper left corner of a single line box.

    Sample:

  PRINT CHR$(218)

STRING$ Function

The STRING$(n,value) will return a string of n occurrences of the character with the ASCII value. Note: value may also be specified as a literal in quotes. For example: STRING$(10,"*") will return a string of 10 asterisks, STRING$(15,42) will return a string of 15 asterisks also, since 42 is the ASCII value of an asterisk.

    Sample:

  PRINT STRING$(n,value)

GRAPHICS

Refer to a QBASIC manual for extra graphic statements and functions that are available.

Examples

The following is a sample formatted screen for the student marks problem, and the code used to generate the screen. Following the approach of Top Down Design, the screen painting has been included in a separate subroutine. Although not normally encouraged, multiple statements may be coded on one physical line by separating them with colons. In normal program logic this usually proves to be confusing for anyone reading the code. In formatted screen painting, it is not uncommon to find multiple statements on a line, especially LOCATE statements followed by PRINT statements. In this case the statements relate to the printing of one or more lines, and multiple statements do not prove to be confusing.

Sample Formatted Screen

```
            ┌─────────────────────────────────────┐
            │    STUDENT PERCENTAGE CALCULATOR    │
            └─────────────────────────────────────┘

    Student's Name
                            *** TEST SCORES***

               Test #1

               Test #2

               Test #1
```

Program To Paint the Screen

```
paintscreen:
   cls
'                                            paint the box
   locate 4,25
   print chr$(218);string$(37,196);chr$(191)
   locate 5,25
   print chr$(179);
   locate 5,63
   print chr$(179)
   locate 6,25
   print chr$(192);string$(37,196);chr$(217)
'                                               box done
   locate 5,30 : print "STUDENT PERCENTAGE CALCULATOR"
   locate 9,13 : print "Student's Name"
   locate 11,35 : print "*** TEST SCORES***"
   locate 14,20 : print "Test #1"
   locate 16,20 : print "Test #2"
   locate 18,20 : print "Test #1"
   return
```

Input Editing on a Formatted Screen

You have probably heard the term "user friendly program." A user friendly program is one that is easy to use, and hard to foul up. From the user's point of view, if a program is prompting her for a number, and the only valid response is between 1 and 10, it would be nice if the program checked her response to ensure that it was indeed between the acceptable limits 1 and 10. If the user's response is not valid then:

- An error message should be displayed.

- A "beep" should be sounded to warn touch typists that an error has occurred (they may not be watching the screen).

- The invalid response should be erased from the screen.

- Prompt for a new response for the same field.

Do not assume that the user's response need only be checked for validity once. Rather, the above actions should be repeatedly performed **until** the user responds with valid data. This implies that there is a need for a controlled loop.

This process is called data validation or input editing. Some fields may require more validation tests than others. For example, a name field would not have an extensive validation check. Perhaps the only check that could be included is that the user does provide a response. This could be validated by ensuring that the contents of the name variable is not null after the INPUT statement.

The following pseudocode is for the portion of the marks program that accepts user input for the first test mark. Valid data must be in the range of 0 to 25 inclusive, because the first test was marked out of 25. Remember that the screen has already been displayed, using the PAINTSCREEN routine illustrated previously. The painted screen includes a prompt area for TEST #1 mark, so the INPUT statement need not include a prompt. The program should position the cursor beside the TEST #1 prompt already displayed on the screen.

Pseudocode

(the paint screen routine has already been executed)
    Position beside the desired prompt already on the screen

Accept the user response

While the response is not valid

    position to the bottom of the screen

    display an error message

    sound a beep

    position back to the user response

    clear the user response from the screen

    position beside the prompt

    accept the user response

end of while loop

clear the error message area (if this point is reached, user must have entered a valid response)

The following is the Basic code to accomplish the validation of the the **first test score** based on the pseudocode above. The code could be modified to input and edit basically any field of data. Suppose the user was responding to a prompt "DO YOU WANT TO DO ANOTHER STUDENT (Y/N)". The Y/N included in the prompt indicates that the user should respond with a Y for yes, or an N for no. User friendly programs will allow the user to respond in upper or lower case.

```
locate 14,29
input "",mark1
while mark1 < 0 or mark1 > 25      'test for bad response
    locate 24,1                    'position to error message line
    print "First test mark must be in the range of 0 to 25";
    beep
    locate 14,29
    print space$(51)               'clear previous response
    locate 14,29
    input "",mark1
wend
locate 24,1                        'position to error message line
print space$(79);                  'clear error message line
```

What would be the condition in the WHILE statement to allow the loop to continue only while the user responds with a bad response?. Typically, programmers get confused as to whether to use AND or OR in the condition. The correct coding of the WHILE statement, assuming that the response has been stored in the variable ANS$, would be:

WHILE ANS$ <> "Y" AND ANS$ <> "N" AND ANS$ <> "y" AND ANS$ <> "n"

Discussion of Code

Several portions of the above code require explanation.

The INPUT statement included a null prompt followed by a comma. This causes Basic to accept input without displaying a prompt or a question mark. This would be desirable when working with formatted input screens.

Old user responses and error messages are erased from the screen by simply printing spaces over the area where the response or message is on the screen.

This program treats the 24th screen line as an error message line. If the program caused printing **beyond** the 24th line, the whole screen would scroll and existing printing on the screen would be forced up one line. If the program includes a formatted screen, then this would throw the alignment off (i.e., the user would expect the prompt TEST #1 to be on line 14, but after scrolling one line it would now be on line 13). For this reason, any PRINT statement on the 24th screen line must end with a semicolon or comma. Recall that ending a PRINT statement with a comma or semicolon suppresses the line feed at the end of the printing. If the line feed is suppressed, then the screen will **not** be forced to scroll up one line.

Review Questions

1. Write a program to allow input of the four coordinates for a box, (Top, Left, Bottom, Right). The program should then use these coordinates to draw a double line box (ASCII Characters: 201, 205, 187, 186, & 188).

2. Write a program for the entry of the amount of a loan. The program must verify that the loan is equal to or greater than $500 and must not exceed $50,000. If the loan exceeds the upper limit, the approval of the branch manger is required. Print an appropriate error message in this case.

3. Write a program to draw a data entry screen for the entry of a customer NAME, ADDRESS, CITY, PROVINCE and POSTAL CODE. The screen should be formated to appear similar to:

```
┌─────────────────────────────────────┐
│                                     │
│        Customer Name.:              │
│                                     │
│        Address............:         │
│                                     │
│        City...............:         │
│                                     │
│        Province .........:          │
│                                     │
│        Postal Code....:             │
│                                     │
└─────────────────────────────────────┘
```

4. Write a short program to allow the user to select where the output of a program will be sent. The program should print the prompt message:

    Output to P)rinter or S)creen?

    and then only allow P or S as valid entries.

CHAPTER 11

Array Processing

Array Processing	**138**
Dimensioning an Array	**139**
Referencing Individual Elements in an Array	**140**
Common Applications of Arrays	**141**
Arrays Used for Lookup	**143**
Loading the Arrays	**143**
Searching the Arrays	**145**
Coding a Search (Table Lookup)	**145**
Review Questions	**147**

Array Processing

Arrays are commonly used to handle large amounts of similar data in an organized manner. A simple one-dimensional array may be thought of as a "list."

In order to appreciate the necessity of arrays, recall how values are stored in memory. Suppose that you have a Basic program that reads a data file to create a report. Are all of the values from the data file in memory at one time? The answer to this is NO. Only one record-worth of data from the file is in memory in variables at one time. When the next record is read, then the values in the variables change. The variables we have used in Basic Programming up to this point have been only capable of storing one value at a time.

Data that are used often during the processing of program (unlike a record in a file that is only required once) would best be stored in memory for the whole duration of the program. A simple example of this would be an application that requires a pay code table as shown below.

PAY CLASS	RATE OF PAY
A10	4.50
C35	9.95
W05	6.60
W10	7.10
G00	12.50

For weekly payroll processing, each employee's record in the data file would contain only the name, the pay class, and the hours worked in the week. In order to calculate the gross pay for each employee (record), the pay class list would have to be searched to find the pay class, and then the appropriate pay rate for that class would be multiplied by the hours worked.

From the above example, it is clear that the pay class list and the pay rate list would have to be used many times in order to calculate pay for employees. Therefore, it is wise to store these values in variables in memory for the duration of the program.

It is also apparent that there are two separate lists of data; pay class, and pay rate. Each list contains data that are similar (related) to the other entries in the list (i.e., all classes, or all rates).

If we were to give each of the five pay classes unique variable names, it would cumbersome (i.e., FIRST.CLASS$, SECOND.CLASS$, etc.). Imagine the number of distinct variable names required, if the company had hundreds of different pay classes.

The alternative is to use an array. An array variable is a multi-dimensional variable. In effect, it is a single variable by name, which has reserved space for many values.

Dimensioning an Array

Extra space must be reserved in memory for array variables. This is done in a DIM statement. DIM is an abbreviation for dimension.

    DIM PAYCLASS$(5), PAYRATE(5)

The number in brackets indicates how many memory locations will be reserved for the array. Therefore, the above statement will set up two variables as arrays in memory, reserving five memory locations for each.

    PAYCLASS$ PAYRATE

Rules for selecting variable names for array variables are just the same as for regular variables. The $ at the end of the array name PAYCLASS$ indicates that it is a string array, capable of storing non-numeric values.

The DIM statement would be included in the program before any reference to the variable is made, so that it is recognized as an array before it is used. For this reason, the most common placement of a DIM statement is either:

   a) at the start of the MAINLINE routine, or

   b) at the start of the INIT routine.

QBASIC automatically assumes a dimension of 10 for any array not dimensioned. As a general rule, however, it is best to be clear to avoid confusion, and always specifically dimension an array using a DIM statement.

Referencing Individual Elements in an Array

In the above example, the variable name PAYCLASS$ refers to an array variable that has five unique memory locations. In order to reference any data in the array, the programmer must specify exactly which of the locations is desired. This is done by the use of a subscript. The subscript is a number in brackets placed after the variable name.

> PAYCLASS$(3) ..... refers to the third memory location in the
> PAYCLASS$ array

Subscripts may be constants, numeric variables, or expressions.

> e.g. PAYCLASS$(3)
> PAYCLASS$(INDX)
> PAYCLASS$(CNT + 2)

Array variables may be used like any other variable, but must **always** include a subscript.

> GROSS.PAY = HOURS * PAYRATE(K)

Problem:

Given a numeric array MARK that has been dimensioned to 30, and contains 30 students marks, what Basic statment(s) would be used to calculate the total of the marks.

Solution 1:

> TOTAL = MARK(1) + MARK(2) + MARK(3) ..... + MARK(30)

This is a very lengthy cumbersome statement. An easier method is to use a loop that repeats 30 times, each time adding the next element in the array to the total.

Solution 2:

```
TOTAL = 0
FOR K = 1 TO 30
    TOTAL = TOTAL + MARK(K)
NEXT K
```

The above solution uses a counted loop. The control variable (K) starts at 1 and is incremented by 1 each time through the loop until the limit of 30 is reached. The control variable is therefore acting exactly as we wish our subscript to, and may therefore be used directly as a subscript.

For the first pass through the loop, the control variable K will contain the value 1. Thus MARK(K) is equivalent to MARK(1) (the first element in the array MARK). For the second pass, K will contain the value 2 and consequently MARK(K) will now point to the second location in the MARK array, and so on.

Combining arrays with loop processing is a powerful tool.

Common Applications of Arrays

A program is to be designed to accept month numbers (1 through 12) and display the appropriate month name (January....etc.).

An array is to be used to store the month names.

    DIM MONTH.NAME$(12)

To print the name of the third month in the array,

    PRINT MONTH.NAME$(3)

The above print statement assumes that the names of the months are already stored in the appropriate locations in the array, MONTH.NAME$.

Recall that at the start of program execution all variables (including arrays) are empty. What statement(s) could be used to store the month names into the array locations?

```
MONTH.NAME$(1) = "January"
MONTH.NAME$(2) = "February"
  etc.
```

This solution would require 12 assignment statements, and a lot of typing. A more common method of storing a list of data values into array locations is using the READ and DATA pair of statements. The data (month names) are provided in a DATA statement commonly placed at the end of a program.

The DATA statement begins with the keyword DATA followed by a list of values separated by commas. Note: string data should be in quotes if it is to include significant spaces, numeric data may not be enclosed in quotes. The number of values provided in one data statement is up to the user, but the values must be in the order required by the program.

```
DATA "January","February","March","April"
DATA "May","June","July","August","September","October"
DATA "November","December"
```

Data statements are commonly located at the physical end of a program. They are non-executable, and merely provide a list of data to be read into variables using a READ statement.

The READ statement, when executed, instructs the computer to fetch the next available value from a DATA statement, and store it into the variable indicated in the READ statement. The following statements would instruct Basic to read the month names in the DATA statement into the first, second, third, etc. locations of the array MONTH.NAME$

```
READ MONTH.NAME$(1)
READ MONTH.NAME$(2)
READ MONTH.NAME$(3)
  etc.
```

This is still cumbersome. It would require 12 READ statements in addition to the DATA statements. Notice the pattern in the subscript however. It starts at 1 and progresses by 1 until a maximum of 12. This would indicate that a counted loop could be used to accomplish the same thing.

```
FOR J = 1 to 12
    READ MONTH.NAME$(J)
NEXT J
```

The process of storing values into array locations, is commonly called **LOADING THE ARRAY** from DATA statement. This action must be performed at the start of the program execution, so that the array contains the required values for the duration of the program. It is therefore performed in the INIT routine.

Arrays Used for Lookup

Loading the Arrays

The first example of arrays presented in this chapter involved two related arrays, PAYCLASS$ and PAYRATE. The first array, PAYCLASS$, would be loaded with all the valid pay classes for a company, and the second array, PAYRATE, would contain the payrate for the PAYCLASS in the same position. These arrays would be dimensioned to five at the start of the program, and loaded with the appropriate data values in the INIT routine. The loading of the arrays could be done in two ways.

Method 1

```
FOR L = 1 TO 5
    READ PAYCLASS$(L)
NEXT L
FOR J = 1 TO 5
    READ PAYRATE(J)
NEXT J
        .
        .
        .
DATA "A10","C35","W05","W10","G00"
DATA  4.50, 9.95, 6.60, 7.10, 12.50
```

Method 2

```
FOR J = 1 TO 5
    READ PAYCLASS$(J), PAYRATE(J)
NEXT J
    .
    .
DATA  "A10",4.50,"C35",9.95,"W05",6.60,"W10",7.10,"G00",12.50
```

Notice that the data to be read are arranged to match the method of loading. In the first method all pay classes are read, and then all rates are read. In the second example, the first class is read, followed by the first rate, then the second class and second rate, etc. Both methods are acceptable, but the second is quicker to execute and requires less code.

Searching the Arrays

After the arrays have been loaded, they may be used in the processing of each data record. In this example, the data file would contain one record for each employee. Each record would contain:

employee number	hours worked	payclass
i.e. 445 ,	10 ,	"W05"

The output required by the program is:

employee number, hours worked, gross pay

In order to manually calculate the gross pay for the above employee, one would have to search the pay class table to find a match between this record's pay class of W05, and an entry in the pay class list. When a match is found (in this case at the third location in the PAYCLASS$ array), the appropriate rate would be used in the same location (the third location in the PAYRATE array). Gross pay for this record would therefore be 66.60 , or (10 * 6.60).

Definitions

The item that is being SEARCHED FOR is called the SEARCH ARGUMENT.

The array being SEARCHED THROUGH is called the ARGUMENT ARRAY.

The array containing the value that we ultimately desire is called the FUNCTION ARRAY.

search argument	argument array	function array
	PAYCLASS	RATE OF PAY
W05	A10	4.50
	C35	9.95
	W05	6.60
	W10	7.10
	G00	12.50

The value from this column.	Is used to search the list in this array for a match.	So that the value from this array can be found.

Coding a Search (Table Lookup)

The process of searching the argument array to find a match with the search argument is coded the same way one would manually perform a search. The search argument is compared with each successive entry in the argument array, starting at the first entry and continuing until a match is found, or the end of the argument array is reached. This process implies the use of a loop to continue stepping through the argument array. The loop should be repeated until a match is found, therefore a DO loop or a WHILE loop is most appropriate. The search process would be performed once for every data record input, and therefore would be included in the process routine.

PROCESS:
```
    INPUT #1, EMPLOYEE.NUM$, EMPLOYEE.HOURS, EMPLOYEE.PAYCLASS$
        ' search PAYCLASS$ array for a match
        ' with EMPLOYEE.PAYCLASS$. Keep stepping
        ' through the array while still less than the
        ' size of array and no match found
    K = 1 ' Set initial index value
    WHILE EMPLOYEE.PAYCLASS$ <> PAYCLASS$(K) AND K < 5
        K = K + 1  ' Increment the index value
    WEND
        ' Loop ends when a match found, or
        ' when end of the array was hit
        ' If a match was found then use the
        ' entry in function array at the
        ' location the match found (K).
        ' If no match was found set gross pay
        ' to zero to indicate an error state.
    IF EMPLOYEE.PAYCLASS$ = PAYCLASS$(K) THEN
        GROSS.PAY = EMPLOYEE.HOURS * PAYRATE(K)
    ELSE
        GROSS.PAY = 0
        PRINT "MISSING PAYCLASS FOR EMPLOYEE";EMPLOYEE.NUM
    END IF
```

Review Questions

1. Write a code segment to read the month names and number of days in the month for each of the 12 months into two arrays called MONTHNM$ and MONTHDAYS. Prepare the DATA statements required for this problem.

2. Write a code segment to ask the user to enter the month number and day number for a date. The program will use the arrays created in question 1 to look up the month name and verify that the day value does not exceed the number of days in the month. Print out an appropriate error message if the user makes a mistake. Note: don't forget to test for valid entry values.

3. Arrays are often used to simplify the problem of accumulating totals when the data must be totaled in catagories. For example, if an accountant had three categories of expenses, 1 - Hardware, 2 - Software, 3 - Miscellaneous and the amounts to be processed each had a code (1, 2 or 3) to signify category, then an array could be used for the accumulators to simplify the process of finding the totals. The category number would be used as the index of the accumultor, to make certain the amount was added to the correct accumulator. The line that would do the accumulation process would be:

    TOTAL(CATEGORY) = TOTAL(CATEGORY) + AMOUNT

    Write a program to allow up to 10 categories of expenses to be used. The program should read a data file with each record containing a category and amount pair of values. The program should print out a report listing the totals for each category.

4. To enhance the program for question 3, add an array that would contain the descriptions for the ten categories. The program should then print out the descriptions for each total in the report.

Problem #1 - Daily Sales Report

INSTRUCTIONS:

A daily sales report is to be prepared for a sporting goods company. Design and code a program in BASIC to produce the report, by reading the sales data from a sequential file and using an in-memory table for inventory data.

INPUT:

Input is a sequential file called "SALTRX" containing the following fields:

- Customer number   - 3 digits
- Invoice Number   - 5 digits
- Product Code   - 5 characters
- Quantity Sold   - 4 digits (numeric)

All data in the file are valid, and will be sorted on invoice number within customer number.

INVENTORY TABLE:

The table is to be loaded into arrays at initialization from DATA statements contained in the program.

```
PRODUCT CODE       PRODUCT DESCRIPTION     PRICE       TAXABLE

B0010              Baseball Today Mag.     1.98        N
B0030              Softball                11.75       Y
B1023              Baseball Bat            28.95       Y
B1030              Hardball                13.70       Y
B9856              Baseball Glove RH       34.98       Y
B9866              Baseball Glove LH       34.98       Y
H0001              N.H.L. News This Week   2.75        N
H0020              Hockey Puck             2.98        Y
H1001              Hockey Stick RH         17.98       Y
H1011              Hockey Stick LH         17.98       Y
H3981              Hockey Skates           78.99       Y
```

OUTPUT:

Using the price obtained from the inventory table via a look up, calculate the sale amount, tax amount and the line total for each record. The tax will be calculated on taxable items at a rate of 15%.

Print a summary at the end of the report, with the grand total sales, tax, and total.

Sample of report layout:

```
06-16-1992                  Jock's Emporium Inc.                    PAGE 1
                            Daily Shipping Report

Customer Invoice
Number   Number   Description         Qty      Sale       Tax       Total
------------------------------------------------------------------------
  423    82356    Baseball Today Mag.   2      3.96      0.00        3.96
  423    82356    Softball             12    141.00     21.15      162.15
  423    82356    Baseball Bat         17    492.15     73.82      565.97
  423    82356    Baseball Glove RH     8    279.84     41.98      321.82
  432    82345    Baseball Bat          3     86.85     13.03       99.88
  432    82345    Hardball             23    315.10     47.27      362.37
  432    82345    Baseball Glove RH     7    244.86     36.73      281.59
  432    82345    Baseball Glove LH     2     69.96     10.49       80.45
  463    98234    Hockey Puck          74    220.52     33.08      253.60
  463    98234    Hockey Stick RH      26    467.48     70.12      537.60
  463    98234    Hockey Stick LH      12    215.76     32.36      248.12
  463    98234    Hockey Skates         2    157.98     23.70      181.68
  463    98392    N.H.L. News This Week 1      2.75      0.00        2.75
  463    98392    Hockey Stick RH       8    143.84     21.58      165.42
  463    98392    Hockey Stick LH      18    323.64     48.55      372.19
                              TOTAL        3,165.69    473.85    3,639.54

                        <--- END OF REPORT --->
```

ENHANCEMENTS:

1. Enhance your program to include single level control breaks such that, on a change of customer number, the totals of sales, tax, and line total are printed.

2. Enhance your program to include two levels of control breaks such that, on a change of invoice number within customer number, the totals of sales, tax, and line total are printed.

3. Enhance your program to only print customer number for the first record for each customer, and to only print invoice number for the first record for each invoice.

```
06-16-1992                  Jock's Emporium Inc.                    PAGE 1
                             Daily Shipping Report
Customer Invoice
Number   Number    Description         Qty      Sale       Tax        Total
-----------------------------------------------------------------------------
  423    82356   Baseball Today Mag.    2       3.96       0.00        3.96
                 Softball              12     141.00      21.15      162.15
                 Baseball Bat          17     492.15      73.82      565.97
                 Baseball Glove RH      8     279.84      41.98      321.82

                 82356 INVOICE TOTAL ----------->   916.95   136.95   1,053.90*

         423 CUSTOMER TOTALS ------------------->   916.95   136.95   1,053.90**

  432    82345   Baseball Bat           3      86.85      13.03       99.88
                 Hardball              23     315.10      47.27      362.37
                 Baseball Glove RH      7     244.86      36.73      281.59
                 Baseball Glove LH      2      69.96      10.49       80.45

                 82345 INVOICE TOTAL ----------->   716.77   107.52     824.29*

         432 CUSTOMER TOTALS ------------------->   716.77   107.52     824.29**

  463    98234   Hockey Puck           74     220.52      33.08      253.60
                 Hockey Stick RH       26     467.48      70.12      537.60
                 Hockey Stick LH       12     215.76      32.36      248.12
                 Hockey Skates          2     157.98      23.70      181.68

                 98234 INVOICE TOTAL ----------->  1,061.74   159.26   1,221.00*

         98392   N.H.L. News This Week  1       2.75       0.00        2.75
                 Hockey Stick RH        8     143.84      21.58      165.42
                 Hockey Stick LH       18     323.64      48.55      372.19

                 98392 INVOICE TOTAL ----------->   470.23    70.12     540.35*

         463 CUSTOMER TOTALS -------------------> 1,531.97   229.38   1,761.35**

                          TOTAL                  3,165.69   473.85   3,639.54***


                        <--- END OF REPORT --->
```

CHAPTER 12

String Manipulation

String Manipulation	**152**
LEFT$ Function	**152**
RIGHT$ Function	**152**
MID$ Function	**153**
LEN Function	**154**
INSTR Function	**154**
STRING$ Function	**155**
SPACE$ Function	**155**
Concatenation	**155**
LINE INPUT Statement	**156**
Numeric Functions and String Functions	**157**
Review Questions	**158**

String Manipulation

Many instances arise in programming where given strings of characters must be separated, rearranged, and combined in different orders. For example, a name field in an input file may be presented in the form JOHN DOE, but on the output report the desired format is DOE, JOHN.

QBASIC provides several functions to parse (pull apart) strings, and to search for given character(s) within strings.

LEFT$ Function

LEFT$ string function will copy the leftmost specified number of characters from a given string. Its format is:

```
LEFT$(source string, number)
```

The source string may be a literal (e.g., "JOHN DOE"), a string variable (e.g., NAM$), or another string function (e.g., LEFT$(X$,2)). The number may be a constant (e.g., 2), a numeric variable (e.g., LAST), or an expression (e.g., A*2+LAST).

Examples:

```
A$ = LEFT$("JOHN DOE",4)      A$ will contain JOHN
X = 1
PRINT  LEFT$(A$,X)            the letter J will print
```

RIGHT$ Function

RIGHT$ string function will copy the rightmost specified number of characters from a given string. Its format is:

```
RIGHT$(source string, number)
```

As with the LEFT$ function, the source string and number parameters may take any of the stated forms.

Chapter 12 String Manipulation 153

Examples:

```
PHONE$ = "(519) 532-1234"
SUFFIX$ = RIGHT$(PHONE$,4)
PRINT SUFFIX$              will print 1234
```

MID$ Function

The MID$ string function (short for MIDDLE) has two different formats. The results depend on the format used.

i) 3 Parameter Format

MID$(source string, start position, number of characters)

This format will copy a sub-string of the source string, starting at the given start character position, and continuing for the number of characters specified. As with the previous functions, the source string may be any string, and the numeric parameters (start position, and number of characters) any number.

Example:

A$ = MID$("abcdefg",3,2)   A$ will contain the portion
                           of the source string starting at
                           the 3rd position, and
                           containing 2 characters.

PROBLEMS: If the starting position parameter given is beyond the end of the string, a null string will be returned. If the number of characters to take is beyond the end of the string, then only as many as exist in the source string will be returned.

ii) 2 Parameter Format

MID$(source string, start position number)

This format will generate a sub-string of the source string starting at the given start character position and continuing to the *end* of the source string. When the third parameter (number of characters to take) is not provided for the MID$ function, it is assumed to continue to the end of the source string. This format of the MID$ function is therefore much like the LEFT$ function, in that it returns the left side of the source string. The difference is that the LEFT$ function returns the leftmost **number** of characters, whereas the

MID$ function returns the leftmost characters **starting at a specified position.**

Example:

    A$=MID$("abcdefg",3)   A$ will contain cdefg

LEN Function

The LEN function (short for length) generates a number that is equal to the length or number of chacters in a given string. Its format is:

    LEN(source string)

As in the previous functions, the source string may take any of the stated forms.

Example:

    NAM$ = "JOHN DOE"
    PRINT LEN(NAM$)   8 will be printed

INSTR Function

The INSTR function (short for IN STRING) will search within a given source string, for a given sub-string. It will generate the number of the character position at which the sub-string was located within the source string, or 0 (zero) if the sub-string was not found.

    INSTR(Start position for search , source string, sub-string)

The start position for search refers to the character in the source string where the search will begin. As with previous functions, the position number to start at may take any numeric form, and the strings may take any string forms.

Example:

    NAM$="DOE, JOHN"
    COMMA.POSITION = INSTR(1, NAM$, ",")
                              COMMA.POSITION will contain 4

If the starting position parameter was given as 5 instead of 1, the variable COMMA.POSITION would contain 0, indicating that the sub-string could not be found. Note that the sub-string could be of any length, and not merely 1 position. For example, the INSTR function could be used to generate the position of a string such as "*****" within a source string.

STRING$ Function

The STRING$ function will generate a string consisting of a specified number of occurrences of a given character.

    STRING$(number of occurrences, character)

Example:

    A$=STRING$(5,"*")   A$ will contain *****

SPACE$ Function

The SPACE$ function will generate a string consisting of a specified number of space characters. This function was introduced in the previous chapter.

    SPACE$(number of occurrences)

Example:

    A$=SPACE$(5)   A$ will contain 5 spaces

Note that the following two functions will generate the same result:

    A$=STRING$(5," ")   A$=SPACE$(5)

Concatenation

Concatenating strings simply means joining together two or more strings to form a single string. Any string may be concatenated with another string (e.g., literals, string variables, and string functions). Concatenation is performed by "adding" two or more strings together using a plus sign (+). Unlike the normal arithmetic interpretation of the plus sign, when used with strings it means join one string to the end of another.

Examples:

    A$ = "ABC" + "DEF"   A$ will contain ABCDEF
    FULL$ = A$ + STRING$(5,".") + "SUSAN"

                                    FULL$ will contain   ABCDEF.....SUSAN

    PRINT   STRING$(3,"Y") + SPACE$(2) + LEFT$(A$,4)

                                      will print   YYY ABCD

LINE INPUT Statement

Recall that the INPUT statement may be used to input data from a data file (INPUT #1,) or from the keyboard interactively (INPUT without a file number parameter). With both versions of the input statement several fields of data may be retrieved with one INPUT statement. The data are provided with a comma to delimit fields. For example:

    INPUT #1, NAM$, ADDRESS$

data from file or user could be

    JOHN DOE, 210 KING ST. KITCHENER ONTARIO

The use of the single comma delimits the two fields of data.

If the user wished to retrieve the whole line of data, ignoring the comma fields delimiters, and treat the whole line of data as one single string, the LINE INPUT statement could be used instead. The end of the input data is identified by the carriage return - line feed combination produced by the ENTER key.

The format of the LINE INPUT statement is:

    LINE INPUT [file#,] string.variable$

Note: The file# is optional, as with the INPUT statement.

Only one string variable may be provided, as the whole line of input will be stored into that single variable regardless of comma delimiters.

Numeric Functions and String Functions

String functions generate strings. As with string variables, string functions always end with a $ sign (e.g., LEFT$, RIGHT$, MID$, SPACE$, STRING$). Numeric functions generate numbers and do not end with a $ sign (e.g., LEN, INSTR).

Sample Problem

A practical example of using several of the string manipulation functions is converting names that are in the form:

>Surname, Given name

to the form:

>Given name Surname

When programming this, you must consider that the same logic must work for all names. Therefore, where the function to extract the last name from the variable NAM$ containing "DOE, JOHN" would be LEFT$(NAM$,3), this would not work if NAM$ contained "LEWIS, JOHN".

Hint: use a function to locate the comma between the names. Then it is obvious that the surname is to the left of the comma, and the given name to the right.

Write the code to perform the above, assuming that the name in the form "Surname, Given" is stored in the variable NAM$, and that the resultant name in the form "Given name Surname" is to be stored in a variable called REVERSED$.

Solution

```
PRINT "Enter A Name in the Format Surname, Given ";
LINE INPUT NAM$
COMMA.POS = INSTR(1,NAM$,",")
GIVENNAME$ = MID$(NAM$,COMMA.POS+1)
SURNAME$ = LEFT$(NAM$, COMMA.POS-1)
REVERSED$ = GIVENNAME$ + " " + SURNAME$
PRINT REVERSED$
```

Review Questions

1. For each of the following, what will be stored in the target variable (i.e., A$) after the statements are executed? Assume that the variable B$ = "Introductory Programming" before execution.

    a)   A$ = LEFT$(B$,4)

    b)   A$ = RIGHT$(B$,11)

    c)   A$ = MID$(B$,14)

    d)   A = LEN(B$)

    e)   SP.LOC = INSTR(1,B$," ")

         A$ = LEFT$(B$, SP.LOC-1)

    f)   A$ = STRING$(5,"-") + MID$(B$,14,7) + STRING$(5,"-")

2. A company uses three part product codes. A hyphen is used to separate the parts of the code. The first part of the code designates the area, the second part the item number, and the third part the type. Write the code segment to print out only the item number portion of any given product code. Use the following product codes to test your solution.

    COB-1365-29   ROOF-11632534-3

PROBLEM #1 - Letter Headers

INSTRUCTIONS:

Create letter headings, given a file containing customer data records.

INPUT:

Input is from the sequential file "CUSTNAME.DAT". Each record in the file contains three fields, separated by commas. The first field is customer name, the second field is customer address, and the third field is a one digit code signifying title.

The name field is in the format: "surname firstname middlename" (each separated by one space) The middle name is optional. Thus if only two portions are given (e.g., RENNER BOB), assume the middle name is missing. You will never be given less that two portions of a name, or more than three.

The address field contains up to three lines of address data. The lines will be separated by a /. e.g.,

"155 King Street/Kitchener Ont./N2A 3A6"

Each line is optional. For example if the address field is:

"255 Dover St./Paris/"

assume that the third line was not provided. If the field is:

"255 Dover St.//Canada"

assume that the second line was not provided. The address field will always contain exactly two delimiters (i.e., slashes).

The third field is a title code. It will be a number between 1 and 6 inclusive. Use the following data to create a table in your program. Load the table from DATA statements.

CODE	TITLE
1	Mrs
2	Mr
3	Miss
4	Ms
5	Rev
6	Dr

OUTPUT:

Create a report of letter headings. Six headings will fit on each page. Allow two blank lines before each letter heading. The letter headings should appear as follows. Generate a

"*** PROCESSING COMPLETE ***"

message at the end of the report.

FORMAT OF OUTPUT:

    title. firstinitial. middleinitial.(leave blank if not provided) surname
    address line 1 leave blank if not provided
    address line 2   "
    address line 3   "
    blank line
    Dear firstname:
    2 blank lines

The following three records would generate output as shown.

    Anthony Susan Beth,122 Krug Place/Kitchener/,1
    Doe John,1677 King St./Waterloo Ontario/H3l T6P,2
    Murphey Paul A,144 Super Ave.//Brantford,5

OUTPUT:

    Mrs. S. B. Anthony
    122 Krug Place
    Kitchener

    Dear Susan:

    Mr. J. Doe
    1677 King St.
    Waterloo Ontario
    H3l T6P

    Dear John:

    Rev P. A. Murphey
    144 Super Ave.

    Brantford

    Dear Paul:

    *** PROCESSING COMPLETE ***

Appendix I

BASIC Reserved Words

$COM1	CLOSE	ERR	LOC	POKE	STRING$
$COM2	CLS	ERROR	LOCAL	POS	SUB
$DEBUG	COLOR	EXIT	LOCATE	PRESET	SWAP
$DYNAMIC	COM	EXP	LOF	PRINT	SYSTEM
$ELSE	COMMAND$	EXP10	LOG	PRINT #	TAB
$ENDIF	COMMON	EXP2	LOG10	PSET	TAN
$EVENT	COS	FIELD	LOG2	PUT	THEN
$IF	CSNG	FILES	LOOP	PUT$	TIME$
$INCLUDE	CSRLIN	FIX	LPOS	RANDOM	TIMER
$INLINE	CVD	FN	LPRINT	RANDOMIZE	TO
$LIST	CVI	FOR	LPRINT #	READ	TROFF
$OPTION	CVL	FRE	LSET	REG	TRON
$SEGMENT	CVMD	GET	MEMSET	REM	UBOUND
$SOUND	CVMS	GET$	MID$	RESET	UCASE$
$STACK	CVS	GOSUB	MKDIR	RESTORE	UNTIL
$STATIC	DATA	GOTO	MKD$	RESUME	USING
ABS	DATE$	HEX$	MKI$	RETURN	USR
ABSOLUTE	DECR	IF	MKL$	RIGHT$	USR0
AND	DEF	IMP	MKMD$	RMDIR	USR1
APPEND	DEFDBL	INCR	MKMS$	RND	USR2
AS	DEFINT	INKEY$	MKS$	RSET	USR3
ASC	DEFLNG	INLINE	MOD	RUN	USR4
AT	DEFSNG	INP	MTIMER	SAVE	USR5
ATN	DEFSTR	INPUT	NAME	SCREEN	USR6
BASE	DELAY	INPUT #	NEXT	SEEK	USR7
BEEP	DIM	INPUT$	NOT	SEG	USR8
BIN$	DO	INSTAT	OCT$	SELECT	USR9
BINARY	DRAW	INSTR	OFF	SERVICE	VAL
BLOAD	DYNAMIC	INT	ON	SGN	VARPTR
BSAVE	ELSE	INTERRUPT	OPEN	SHARED	VARPTR$
CALL	ELSEIF	IOCTL	OPTION	SHELL	VARSEG
CASE	END	IOCTL$	OR	SIN	VIEW
CDBL	ENDMEM	KEY	OUT	SOUND	WAIT
CEIL	ENVIRON	KILL	OUTPUT	SPACE$	WEND
CHAIN	ENVIRON$	LBOUND	PAINT	SPC	WHILE
CHDIR	EOF	LCASE$	PALETTE	SQR	WIDTH
CHR$	EQV	LEFT$	PALETTE USING	STATIC	WINDOW
CINT	ERADR	LEN	PEEK	STEP	WRITE
CIRCLE	ERASE	LET	PEN	STICK	WRITE #
CLEAR	ERDEV	LINE	PLAY	STOP	XOR
CLNG	ERDEV$	LIST	PMAP	STR$	
	ERL		POINT	STRIG	

Appendix II

ASCII Character Codes

0	NUL	32		64	@	96	`	128	Ç	160	á	192	└	224	α
1	☺	33	!	65	A	97	a	129	ü	161	í	193	┴	225	β
2	●	34	"	66	B	98	b	130	é	162	ó	194	┬	226	Γ
3	♥	35	#	67	C	99	c	131	â	163	ú	195	├	227	π
4	♦	36	$	68	D	100	d	132	ä	164	ñ	196	─	228	Σ
5	♣	37	%	69	E	101	e	133	à	165	Ñ	197	┼	229	σ
6	♠	38	&	70	F	102	f	134	å	166	ª	198	╞	230	µ
7	BEL	39	'	71	G	103	g	135	ç	167	º	199	╟	231	τ
8	BS	40	(	72	H	104	h	136	ê	168	¿	200	╚	232	Φ
9	HT	41	)	73	I	105	i	137	ë	169	⌐	201	╔	233	Θ
10	LF	42	*	74	J	106	j	138	è	170	¬	202	╩	234	Ω
11	VT	43	+	75	K	107	k	139	ï	171	½	203	╦	235	δ
12	FF	44	,	76	L	108	l	140	î	172	¼	204	╠	236	∞
13	CR	45	-	77	M	109	m	141	ì	173	¡	205	═	237	φ
14	SO	46	.	78	N	110	n	142	Ä	174	«	206	╬	238	ε
15	SI	47	/	79	O	111	o	143	Å	175	»	207	╧	239	∩
16	►	48	0	80	P	112	p	144	É	176	░	208	╨	240	≡
17	◄	49	1	81	Q	113	q	145	æ	177	▒	209	╤	241	±
18	↕	50	2	82	R	114	r	146	Æ	178	▓	210	╥	242	≥
19	‼	51	3	83	S	115	s	147	ô	179	│	211	╙	243	≤
20	¶	52	4	84	T	116	t	148	ö	180	┤	212	╘	244	⌠
21	§	53	5	85	U	117	u	149	ò	181	╡	213	╒	245	⌡
22	▬	54	6	86	V	118	v	150	û	182	╢	214	╓	246	÷
23	↨	55	7	87	W	119	w	151	ù	183	╖	215	╫	247	≈
24	↑	56	8	88	X	120	x	152	ÿ	184	╕	216	╪	248	°
25	↓	57	9	89	Y	121	y	153	Ö	185	╣	217	┘	249	·
26	→	58	:	90	Z	122	z	154	Ü	186	║	218	┌	250	·
27	ESC	59	;	91	[	123	{	155	¢	187	╗	219	█	251	√
28	∟	60	<	92	\	124	|	156	£	188	╝	220	▄	252	ⁿ
29	GS	61	=	93	]	125	}	157	¥	189	╜	221	▌	253	²
30	RS	62	>	94	^	126	~	158	₧	190	╛	222	▐	254	■
31	US	63	?	95	_	127	⌂	159	ƒ	191	┐	223	▀	255	

Line Draw Characters

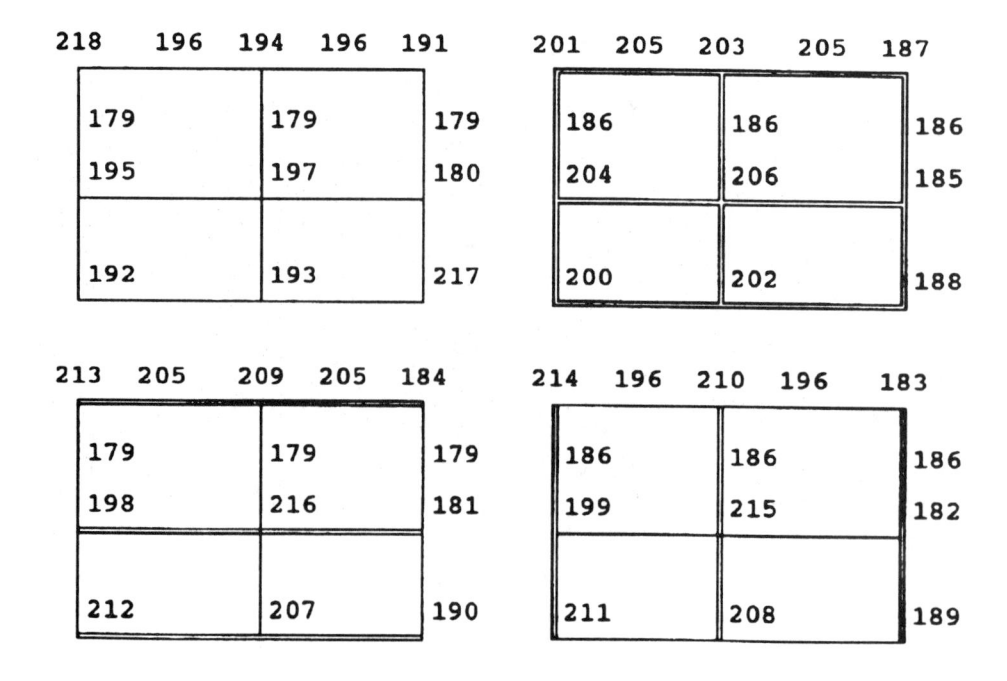

```
  218   196   194   196   191        201   205   203   205   187
   ┌─────┬─────┐                       ╔═════╦═════╗
   │ 179 │ 179 │ 179                   ║ 186 ║ 186 ║ 186
   │ 195 │ 197 │ 180                   ║ 204 ║ 206 ║ 185
   ├─────┼─────┤                       ╠═════╬═════╣
   │ 192 │ 193 │ 217                   ║ 200 ║ 202 ║ 188
   └─────┴─────┘                       ╚═════╩═════╝

  213   205   209   205   184        214   196   210   196   183
   ╒═════╤═════╕                       ╓─────╥─────╖
   │ 179 │ 179 │ 179                   ║ 186 ║ 186 ║ 186
   │ 198 │ 216 │ 181                   ║ 199 ║ 215 ║ 182
   ╞═════╪═════╡                       ╟─────╫─────╢
   │ 212 │ 207 │ 190                   ║ 211 ║ 208 ║ 189
   ╘═════╧═════╛                       ╙─────╨─────╜
```

Appendix III

The QBASIC System

QBASIC is started by entering the command QBASIC and then pressing **Enter**. After a few moments the QBASIC opening screen will appear.

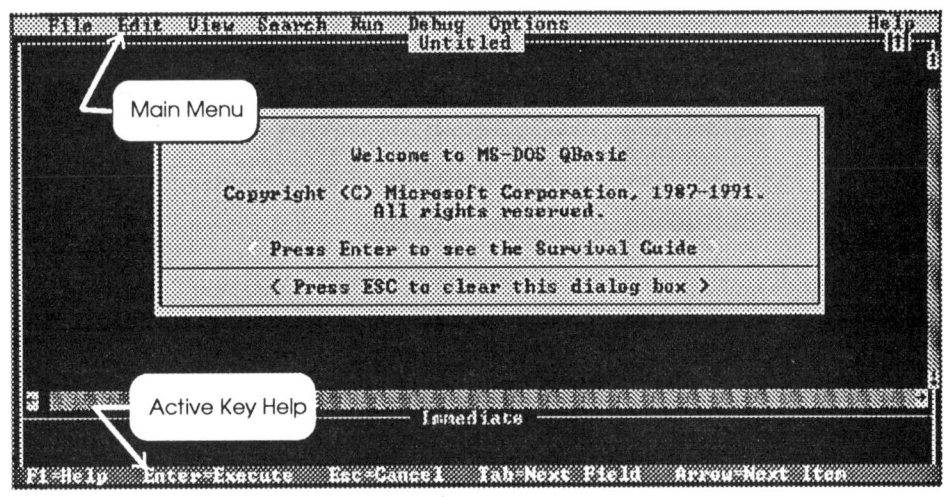

Figure 1 - QBASIC Opening Screen

The opening screen has a dialogue box (a box containing an information message). If you press **Enter**, then the Survival Guide for QBASIC will begin. The Survival Guide is an on-line tutorial for QBASIC. Press the **Esc** key and the dialogue box is cleared. The cursor will be in the edit window, ready to begin entering a program. At this time press **Esc**, so that we can explore the edit screen.

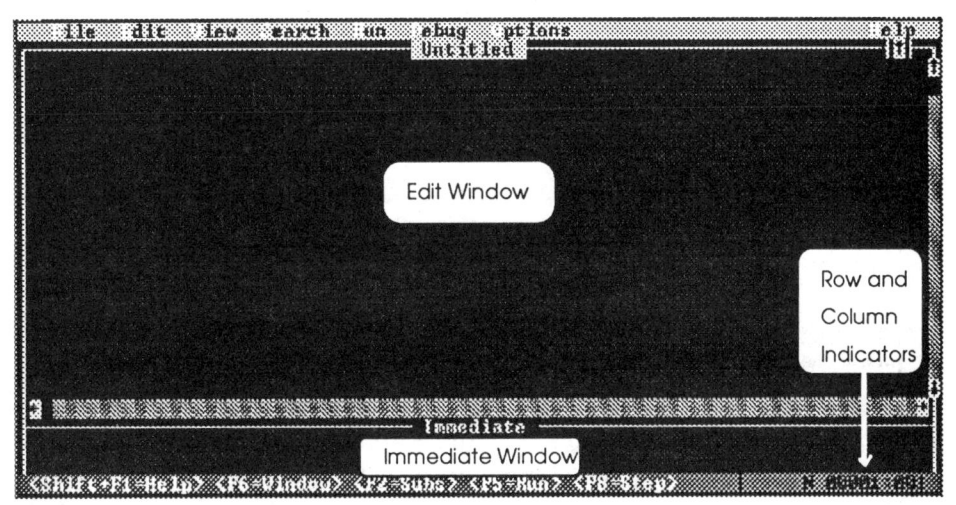

Figure 2 - Edit Screen

The Edit Window

At the center top of the Edit window is the word UNTITLED. This represents the name of the file that is being edited. Since we have not created a file, the initial name is Untitled. A flashing underscore (_) is the cursor indicating the position where the next character will be entered. If you have not entered any text, the cursor will be in the upper left corner of the Edit Window. Enter your name. Notice the Row and Column indicators in the lower right corner of the screen. These numbers will change as you enter your name, to indicate the row and column position of the cursor. Now that you have entered your name, the cursor control keys (⇐ ⇑ ⇓ ⇒) can be used to move the cursor to any point in the text.

Overwrite or Insert Modes:

Initially the editor is in the **Overwrite** mode, which means that if you position the cursor in the middle of some text and begin to type, the entered text replaces (overwrites) the old text. You can change the mode to **Insert** mode by pressing the **Insert** key. In insert mode, the cursor changes to a flashing box. When text is entered, it is inserted and the old text is pushed to the right. You can switch back to the overwrite mode by pressing the **Insert** key, and the cursor returns to the flashing underscore.

The Immediate Window

The small window at the bottom of the screen is called the Immediate Window. Its purpose is to allow the entry of QBASIC instructions that will be executed immediately. You will often use the `CLS` command in this window to clear the output window. To switch between the Edit and Immediate windows, press the **F6** function key.

The Run Window

The Run Window is actually the full screen. Each time you run a program, the results will be displayed on the run window. You can switch between the Edit Screen and the Run window by pressing the **F4** function key.

Editing A Program

The QBASIC editor provides all of the commands required to enter the code for a program. Use upper or lower case letters when typing in your program. QBASIC will switch all BASIC keywords to upper case (capitals) when you press the **Enter** key to end the line. If you follow the practice (highly recommended) of indenting the contents of loops and If's, QBASIC will indent the next lines entered.

Making Corrections

The **Del** key and the **Backspace** keys can both be used to erase characters from the line. The **Del** key removes the character at the cursor position, the **Backspace** removes the character to the left of the cursor.
A complete line can be erased by placing the cursor anywhere in the line and pressing **Ctrl + Y** (Hold down **Ctrl** and press **Y**).

Moving The Cursor

The cursor arrow keys move the cursor through the entered text as you might expect.
Left and Right arrow keys (⇐ ⇒) move one character left or right.
Up and Down arrow keys (⇑ ⇓) move cursor one line up or down.
Page Up and **Page Down** move one complete screen through the file.
End moves the cursor to the end of the current line.
Home moves the cursor to the first character in the line.
Ctrl + END moves cursor to the last line in the program file.
Ctrl + HOME moves cursor to the first line in the file.

The MAIN MENU

The main menu across the top of the screen provides the selections:

File Edit View Search Run Debug Options Help

You activate the main menu by pressing the **Alt** key. When you hold the **Alt** key down, the first letter of each choice changes colour. When you release the **Alt** key, the first word will be highlighted with a black background. The black background indicates that the menu is ACTIVE and you may use the left (⇐) and right (⇒) cursor control keys to move the black background from choice to choice. Pressing either the Up (⇑) or Down (⇓) keys will make the Pull Down menus appear. The pull down menus list the sub-choices for each of the main menu selections. Once you are familiar with the menu choices, you can make a quick selection by holding down the **Alt** key and pressing the first letter of the menu selection. For example, if you wish to select the File option, hold down **Alt** and press **F**.

166   Appendix III

The Active Key Help Line

At the very bottom of the screen is a line listing a number of keys that will perform special functions. This line is a help line to remind you about which special Keys are active and what action the keys perform. The keys that perform special functions may change, depending upon what stage you are in using QBASIC, thus this line will change from time to time. The help line for the Opening Screen tells you that the **Esc** key is used to cancel (Escape from) a command. You can use the **Esc** key to cancel the menu if you made it active by accident.

The File Sub-Menu

New   This choice clears the edit window and starts a new untitled file.

Open   This choice will display the file open dialogue box, which you can use to select the file that you wish to edit. Use the **Tab** key while in the Open dialogue box to move from section to section. Each time you press **Tab** the cursor will cycle through the File Name, Files, Dirs/Drives and command sections of the dialogue box. When you have moved to the section required, press the up or down (⇑ ⇓) keys to select the choice from the list, then press **Enter** to select.

Save   This selection will save the file being edited. If the file is untitled, a dialogue box will appear and allow you to enter a name.

Save As Use this selection to save a file with a new name. It will always bring up the dialogue box used to rename the untitled files.

Print   Use this selection to print a copy of the file being edited. When selected, a dialogue box can be used to print Selected text, Current Window or Entire File. The box defaults to the entire file but you can use the cursor keys to select the other choices.

Exit   Used to exit the program and return to the DOS prompt.

The Edit Sub-Menu

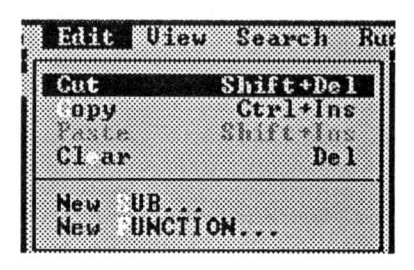

The editor can be used to make large changes to the file by using the cut and paste method. You can use these editing methods to delete, copy or move large sections of a program. The first step in using these commands is to mark the text to be deleted, copied or moved.

Marking

Text Move the cursor to the beginning of the section of text to be marked. Then while holding down the **Shift** key, use the cursor movement keys to expand the highlight colour until all of the text to be marked is highlighted. Then release the **Shift** key. The text will remain marked until you are finished with the cut and paste process or until you press another key.

Cut This selection is used to remove the marked text from the file. The text is placed in temporary storage (the clipboard) so that it can be retrieved by the Paste command.

Copy This selection will copy the marked text to the clipboard, but in this case the original copy is still in the file.

Paste This command will insert the contents of the clipboard into the file beginning at the current cursor position.

The remaining selection from the sub-menu are not required for this introductory course and will not be covered here. If you wish to explore them further, use the on line help and tutorials.

The View Sub-Menu

SUBs This command is related to the New SUB commands in the Edit sub-menu. It's purpose is for selecting the section of a large program that you wish to edit.

Split This command will split the edit window into two halves. The current program will appear in both windows so this selection is very useful when you want to simultaniously look at two sections of the program. Use the **F6** function key to switch between the windows.

Output Screen This command can be used in place of the **F4** function key to switch to the output screen.

The Search Sub-Menu

Find Use this selection to search the file for a word or character pattern. This process is very useful when looking for the occurences of a particular variable name or key word. The search begins at the current cursor position. Use **Ctrl + Home** first if you wish to begin at the start of the file.

Repeat Last Find Used to repeat the last find that was entered. This can be used even if you have left the search sub-menu and returned to it later.

Change This command is useful if you which to change all occurances of a pattern with a new pattern. Useful for changing the PRINT key word to LPRINT when ready to test the printing to the printer. The search for the Change begins at the current cursor position (see Find).

The Run Sub-Menu

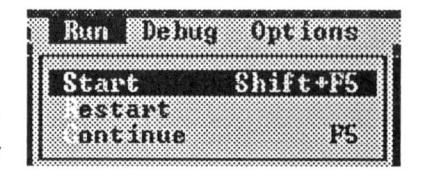

Start Used to begin executing the program. Can also use the **Shift + F5** key combination.

Restart Used to restart a program halted by the debug process.

Continue Continues executing a program from the currently highlighted statement. This command is useful when a debug command has halted the execution of the program. The command can also be given by pressing the **F5** function key.

The Debug Sub-Menu

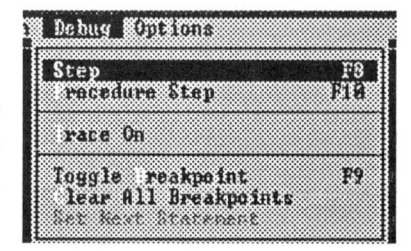

Debugging a program is a skill that anyone who aspires to be a programmer must learn. There are two stages in debugging a program. The first is easy to master, the second is much more difficult.

The first stage is clearing the "syntax errors" that occur when typing the program. Syntax errors are caused by incorrect statements due to misspelled keywords, missing or incorrect parameters, etc. QBASIC detects these errors as the statements are entered. A few errors due to misspelled variable names may not be noticed until the program is run, then the error is detected when the program stops unexpectedly with an error message. The errors that occur when the program is executed are often caused by undefined variables or variables containing the wrong type of data.

The second stage in debugging occurs after all of the fatal errors have been cleared. Second stage errors do not cause the program to stop executing; they simply result in incorrect solutions. Programmers must be very careful to test the program to make certain that it handles all of the unusual data values. Second stage errors are the most dificult to detect. The various debug commands are most useful for detecting second stage errors.

For this second stage of debugging it is very useful if the programmer can watch the statements of the program as they are executed. This can be accomplished by Stepping through the statements slowly, executing the statements one at a time, so that the results of each statement can be examined before the next one executes.

The trace process can be useful, since the programmer can watch the statements as they execute. This process is useful for detecting logic errors that cause the program to execute incorrect sections.

Another useful debugging tool is the breakpoint. A breakpoint is a statement marked as a stopping point. When the program reaches this statement, it automatically stops executing (break) and returns to the edit screen. The breakpoint is very useful for stopping the program just before the area suspected of containing the error executes. Once the program is halted, the step process can be used to slowly work through the statements, looking for the cause of the error. While the program is interrupted, the programmer can examine the data stored in variables by using the print statement in the Immediate screen.

The QBASIC debug sub-menu provides most of the useful debugging tools and will be very useful for tracking down those elusive "bugs."

Step Use this command or the **F8** function key to make the program execute a single statement. Each time the command is given, the program proceeds one statement further through the program. After each statement the process returns to the edit screen where the immediate window can be used to examine the data stored in variables.

Procedure
Step This command or **F10** is used to run each procedure (subprog), and then halt execution when the procedure is completed. Use this command before the single step process, to find the procedure that has seems to be causing the problem.

Trace On This selection is used to turn on or off the tracing of executing statements. When turned on, the process highlights each statement as it executes.

Toggle Break
Points This command is used to set or clear single break points. To set a break point, move the edit cursor to the statement and then use this menu selection to mark the break point. To clear a break point, move the edit cursor to the breakpoint line and then use this command or **F9** to clear the breakpoint.

Clear All
Breakpoints Use to clear (remove) all breakpoints set in the program.

Set Next
Statement Is used when a program has been interrupted during execution. Move the edit cursor to the line where you wish the program to begin executing, and then make this menu selection.

Index

A

Accumulating	33
Algorithm	6, 7
AND Operator	59
Application of Arrays	141
Argument Array	145
Array	
One-Dimension	138
Array Processing	138
Array Variable Names	139
ASCII	131
ASCII Character Codes	162
Assignment Statement	21
Auxiliary Storage	ii

B

BASIC	2
Statements	15
BASIC Commands	
EDIT	2
LOAD	2
RUN	2
SAVE	2
BASIC Reserved Words	161

C

CHR$ Function	131
CLS Statement	129
Color Codes	130
COLOR Statement	130
Compiler	iii
Compound Logical Expressions	59
Concatenation	155
Conditional	54
Conditional Processing	48
Control	
Break	101
Field	101
Group	101
Total	101
Control Break	
Detecting	102
Controlled Loop	133
Counted Loop	141
Counted Loops	120
Counters83	
Counting	33
Counts	33
CPU	ii

D

Data File	17
DATA Statement	142
DATE$ Function	71
Debug	25
Decision Process	38
Detail Lines	82
DIM Statement	139
Dimension	139
Disk Drive	ii
DO Statement	23
DOS	iii

E

Edit Mask	71
Edit Mask Code	
# (Numeric Digit)	72
$ (Dollar Fill)	73
* (Asterisk Fill)	73
, (Comma)	72
- (Minus)	74
\ (Backslash)	74
Edit Masks	
Combined	75
Separate Coding	76
End of File	24
END Statement	24
EOF() Function	24
Error	
Type Mismatch Error	21
Error Message	133

F

False Control Break	107
Files	2
Extension	3
File Extension	2
File Name	2

Filename	2, 3
Flowchart	6, 39, 77
Flowcharting	38
FOR Statement	121
Form Feed	84
Formatted Screens	129
Function Array	145

G

GOSUB Statement	16
GRAPHICS	131
Group Totals	100, 103

H

Hardware	i
Heading Lines	82
Headings	31
High Level Language	iv

I

IF Statement	48
Nested	55
Initialization	8, 10
Input	18
Input Devices	ii
Input Editing	133
Input Process	38
INPUT Statement	20, 128
INSTR Function	154
Integer Arithmetic	97
Integer Division	96
Interpreter	iii
Interractive Programming	127

K

Keyword	15

L

Label	16
Label Names	17
Last Group Total Missing	108
LEFT$ Function	152
LEN Function	154
LET Statement	21, 22

Line Counter	83
Line Draw Characters	162
LINE INPUT Statement	156
Lists of Data	138
Literal	152
Loading the Array	143
Locate Statement	129
Logic	4
Logic Errors	6
Logical Expression	49
Logical Operators	59
Lookup Table	
Searching	144
Lookup Table Processing	143
Loop	
Counted	120, 141
DO/ LOOP Type	118
FOR/ NEXT Type	121
Nested	123
WHILE/ WEND Type	120
LOOP Statement	23
Looping	4, 10, 23, 118
LPRINT Statement	22

M

Machine Language	iii
Main Memory	ii
Mainline	8, 9
MID$ Function	153
MOD Operator	96
Modules	8

N

Nested IF Statements	55
Nested Loops	123
Networking	i
NEXT Statement	121
Numeric Variables	19

O

OPEN Statement	17
Operator	
Logical	59
MOD	96
Operators	
Arithmetic	21
Integer Division	96
Relational	49
OR Logical Operator	59

Order of Operations	22
Output	22
Output Devices	ii
Output Process	38

P

Page Break	82
Page Counter	83
Page Eject	84
Page Full - Detecting	83
Page Headings	84
Page Layout	82
Predefined Process	38
PRINT Statement	22
Ends With Comma or Semicolon	69
PRINT USING Statement	71
Print Zones	22
Process	8, 10, 38
Processor or CPU	ii
Program	iv
Program Logic	54
Programming Standards	16
Prompt	128
Pseudocode	6, 9, 32, 34, 77, 86, 105, 109, 133

Q

QBASIC	2
Quotes	23

R

READ Statement	142
Relational Operators	49
REM Statement	15
Repeditive Process	38
Report Headings	31
Report Layout	69, 77
Report Totals	31, 104
RETURN Statement	16
RIGHT$ Function	152
Routines	8

S

Screen Painting	129
Search Argument	145
Selection	10
Selection Structure	48
Sequence	10
Sequential Data File	101
Significant Digits	94
Software	iii
Sort	101
SPACE$ Function	130, 155
SPC Function	70
Standard Page	83
Standards	16
Statement	iv
String Manipulation	152
String Variables	19, 20
STRING$ Function	131, 155
Strings	74
Structured Programming	10
Subscript	140
Sum of Sum Logic	104
Summary Lines	82
Summary Totals	33
Syntax	iv
Syntax Errors	6

T

TAB Function	70
Table Lookup	145
Table Searching	144
Tables	138
Termination	8, 10
Top Down Design	7, 16, 84, 131
Totals	31, 33
Group	100, 103
Report	104
Type Mismatch Error	21

U

User Friendly	133

V

Variable	10, 18
Names	19
Numeric	93
Save	103
String	93
Types	19
Variable Types	93
Variables	33
Accumulators	33
Array	139

Counters	33
Double Precision	94
Integer	93
Single Precision	94
Video Screen Size	129
Visual Table of Contents	8, 86, 105

W

WEND Statememt	120
WHILE Statement	120